VICTIMIZATION AND FEAR OF CRIME AMONG THE ELDERLY

by

Yves Brillon

International Centre for Comparative Criminology
University of Montreal

(Translated by D. R. Crelinsten)

Butterworths
Toronto and Vancouver

Victimization and Fear of Crime Among the Elderly
English language edition © 1987 Butterworths, A division of Reed Inc.

Printed and bound in Canada

The Butterworth Group of Companies

Canada
Butterworths, Toronto and Vancouver

United Kingdom
Butterworth & Co. (Publishers) Ltd., London and Edinburgh

Australia
Butterworth Pty Ltd., Sydney, Melbourne, Brisbane, Adelaide and Perth

New Zealand
Butterworths (New Zealand) Ltd., Wellington and Auckland

Singapore
Butterworth & Co. (Asia) Pte. Ltd., Singapore

South Africa
Butterworth Publishers (SA) (Pty) Ltd., Durban and Pretoria

United States
Butterworth Legal Publishers, Boston, Seattle, Austin and St. Paul
D&S Publishers, Clearwater

Canadian Cataloguing in Publication Data

Brillon, Yves
 Victimization and fear of crime among the elderly

(Perspectives on individual and population aging)
Bibliography: p.
Includes index.
ISBN 0-409-81025-8

1. Aged – Canada – Crimes against. 2. Aged –
Canada – Abuse of. 3. Aged – Canada – Attitudes.
4. Victims of crimes – Canada. I. Title. II. Series.

HV6250.4.A34B74 1987   362.8'8'0880565   C87-093666-2

Executive Editor (P. & A.): Lebby Hines
Sponsoring Editor: Janet Turner
Managing Editor: Linda Kee
Supervisory Editor: Marie Graham
Editor: Priscilla Darrell
Cover Design: Patrick Ng
Production: Jill Thomson

To my wife Brigitte

And to our daughters Pascale and Laurence

BUTTERWORTHS PERSPECTIVES ON INDIVIDUAL AND POPULATION AGING SERIES

The initiation of this Series represents an exciting and significant development for gerontology in Canada. Since the production of Canadian-based
knowledge about individual and population aging is expanding rapidly,
students, scholars and practitioners are seeking comprehensive yet succinct
summaries of the literature on specific topics. Recognizing the common
need of this diverse community of gerontologists, Janet Turner, Sponsoring
Editor at Butterworths, conceived the idea of a series of specialized
monographs that could be used in gerontology courses to complement existing texts and, at the same time, to serve as a valuable reference for those
initiating research, developing policies, or providing services to elderly
Canadians.

Each monograph includes a state-of-the-art review and analysis of the
Canadian-based scientific and professional knowledge on the topic. Where
appropriate for comparative purposes, information from other countries is
introduced. In addition, some important policy and program implications
of the current knowledge base are discussed, and unanswered policy and
research questions are raised to stimulate further work in the area. The
monographs have been written for a wide audience: undergraduate students
in a variety of gerontology courses; graduate students and research personnel who need a summary and analysis of the Canadian literature prior to initiating research projects; practitioners who are involved in the daily planning and delivery of services to aging adults; and policy-makers who
require current and reliable information in order to design, implement and
evaluate policies and legislation for an aging population.

The decision to publish a monograph on a specific topic has been based in
part on the relevance of the topic for the academic and professional community, as well as on the extent of information available at the time an
author is signed to a contract. Thus, not all the conceivable topics are included in the early stages of the Series and some topics are published earlier
rather than later. Because gerontology in Canada is attracting large
numbers of highly qualified graduate students as well as increasingly active
research personnel in academic, public and private settings, new areas of
concentrated research will evolve. Hence, additional monographs that
review and analyze work in these areas will be needed to reflect the evolu-

tion of knowledge on specialized topics pertaining to individual or population aging in Canada.

Before introducing the fourth monograph in the Series, I would like, on behalf of the Series' authors and the gerontology community, to acknowledge the following members of the Butterworths "team" and their respective staffs for their unique and sincere contribution to gerontology in Canada: Geoffrey Burn, President, for his continuing support of the project despite difficult times in the Canadian publishing industry; Janet Turner, Sponsoring Editor, for her vision, endurance and high academic standards; Linda Kee, Managing Editor, for her coordination of the production, especially her constant reminders to authors (and the Series Editor) that the hands of the clock continue to move in spite of our perceptions that manuscript deadlines were still months or years away; Jim Shepherd, Production Manager, for nimbly vaulting many a technical obstacle; and Gloria Vitale, Academic Sales Manager, for her support and promotion of the Series. For each of you, we hope the knowledge provided in this Series will have personal value — but not until well into the next century!

Barry D. McPherson
Series Editor

FOREWORD

Any consumer of the mass media can likely recall viewing, listening to, or reading about a particularly tragic story involving an elderly person who was physically attacked or who was the victim of fraud, property damage or mental abuse. One outcome of this media exposure is that some elderly people begin to perceive their environment as unsafe and to fear that they will be personally victimized. Another consequence is that, regardless of age, the general public believes that elderly persons, especially older women, are frequent victims of criminal acts or abuse, and that this segment of the population has reason to live in fear. Yet, data from numerous countries document that there is a sharp decline in the reported rates of personal and violent victimization among successively older age groups. In fact, it is those between about 16 and 24 years of age who tend to be victimized most frequently. In contrast, the reported rates for fear of crime seem to increase among successively older age groups.

As a result of growing interest in the quality of life of our aging population, and because of the reaction to media reports concerning the victimization of older adults, scholars and practitioners have initiated research, policy analyses and social programs concerning societal and domestic violence against older adults. Specifically, the focus has been on such issues as the incidence of victimization, the consequences of victimization, the attitudes and concerns of older adults towards crime (*i.e.*, fear of crime), and the neglect and abuse of the elderly within the family or in a long-term care institution. This research is concerned with whether the quality of life of older adults deteriorates, either because they are victimized or, more likely, because they fear victimization and isolate themselves, thereby becoming "a prisoner in their own home". Furthermore, research has sought to understand whether this fear of crime leads to a decline in well-being and life satisfaction (*e.g.*, depression); to an unfounded suspicion of neighbours, strangers and youths; to a forced relocation; or, to social involvement only during the daylight hours.

Professor Brillon critically reviews the literature on crime and aging to provide answers to these questions for students, social workers, gerontologists, criminologists, the research community, and government and law enforcement personnel. Throughout the monograph, Canadian data are compared with patterns found in other countries, particularly the United States and Great Britain.

In Chapter 1, the reader is introduced to the general issue of crime and violence and how both actual victimization and fear of crime can influence the quality and style of life of older Canadians. Chapter 2, stressing the heterogeneity of the elderly population, illustrates how the vulnerability of the elderly to acts of crime can vary by such factors as health and economic status. Similarly, Chapter 3 identifies the factors related to variation in the perceived fear of crime among the elderly, and presents the beliefs of elderly Canadians about criminals and the criminal justice system. As noted by the author, many of the perceptions and fears held by the elderly are based on media reports of incidents that often occur elsewhere in the country, rather than on personal experience as a victim, or on knowing a victim in their own neighbourhood or community.

In the next two chapters, the incidence of and inter-relationship between rates of victimization and fear of crime are described and discussed. As in other countries, even where there is a low rate of elder victimization, there is a high rate of fear, especially among elderly women. These chapters include a discussion of the consequences of experiencing either actual victimization or the fear of being victimized. In addition, Professor Brillon discusses the effect of possible confounding variables, and offers alternative explanations as to why the elderly are victimized less, yet report higher levels of fear of crime.

Chapter 6 introduces the reader to a heretofore "hidden" social problem, the neglect and abuse of the elderly person. While not a "crime" in the legal sense (unless the victim is physically abused or subjected to fraudulent behaviour), incidents are increasingly being reported within both family and institutional settings. To sensitize the reader to this problem, the hypothesized causes of elder abuse are summarized and reviewed. The final chapter identifies a number of policy and research questions that must be addressed in the near future by the research, social welfare and volunteer communities.

In conclusion, this is a timely and important monograph. We know relatively little about victimization, abuse, or fear of crime among the elderly in Canada. An increase in knowledge about crime and aging is especially necessary to maintain or enhance the quality of life of older Canadians. We hope that this monograph will stimulate research that will expand our knowledge base concerning patterns and trends in domestic, institutional and societal crimes against the elderly; and, about the dynamics and consequences of fear among the elderly. At the same time, there is an urgent need to incorporate this knowledge base into policy and evaluation research to assess the effectiveness of programs and policies designed to alleviate the present level of fear of crime, and to alter the settings which predispose an elderly person to indirect or direct forms of physical, economic or psychological abuse.

Barry D. McPherson, Ph.D.
Series Editor
Waterloo, Ontario, Canada
May, 1987

PREFACE

"It is not enough to add years to life,
but we must add life to years."
(John F. Kennedy)

Since the 60s, research on how the public views the criminal justice system
has proliferated to such an extent that, in Kegel's words, "crime seems to be
at the top of the hit-parade of opinion polls today" (1982, p. 210). This
tremendous interest in public opinion studies, however, is not accidental or
untimely. It is largely because of the inability of the penal agencies to effectively limit crime that researchers have turned their attention directly to the
people. By doing so, they were able to:

(1) better evaluate the nature and extent of the actual crime situation;
(2) to ascertain the influence of crime and victimization on people's
attitudes and behaviour;
(3) to analyse the public's attitude toward justice as well as toward the
objectives and functioning of the various penal agencies.

As portrayed daily by the media, violence is everywhere and crime is
increasing. Our modern oracles, the surveys, judge the consequences of this
apparent increase in violence by the general fear it engenders and, at the
same time, take this fear as a measure of the increase in violence. "In other
words, the apparent increase in fear among the people is supposed to reflect
the actual amount of violence, to reveal the true facts" (Louis-Guérin 1983).
For the individual, fear can become a cause of distress, restriction and
withdrawal, especially for persons who feel vulnerable, as may be the case
for some elderly citizens. For the group, it can lead to defensive behaviour,
intolerance and punitiveness.

In this monograph, the principal Canadian studies that have been completed on elderly persons with regard to victimization, fear of crime and
abuse are reviewed. There is no work to date that collects and summarizes
the data and conclusions of this body of research. A work of this kind
should encourage further research. Science is a cumulative process; it involves a knowledge and analysis of results already acquired in order to
stimulate further investigation. In writing this book, my only interest was
to give an account of the most important studies on violence and its consequences for senior citizens. Unfortunately, there was very little Canadian

research in this field. Moreover, that which has been completed is not well known, having been given limited distribution and publication in many cases.

Despite certain gaps or perhaps omissions, this monograph should be extremely useful to all who are interested in the quality of life of the elderly and, more particularly, in the violence perpetrated against this age group. Also, it should give undergraduate students, practitioners and policy-makers the most salient facts that, in Canada, describe crimes of violence against elderly citizens as well as the influence they have on their living conditions, their behaviour and their attitudes. Since there is often little Canadian material that is pertinent, reference is made to American research, where helpful, in order to establish comparisons or to point to scientific data that needed to be acquired, verified or studied more deeply in Canada. We trust this book will be of use to all who work with the elderly and are concerned about their fate, that it will make a worthy contribution to the expansion of criminological research on our senior citizens and that it will encourage people to think more about the conditions of life for the aged.

ACKNOWLEDGEMENTS

It gives me great pleasure to be a contributor to the Butterworth series, *Perspectives on Individual and Population Aging*. This monograph, *Victimization and Fear of Crime among the Elderly*, is being published thanks to Professor Barry D. McPherson who was kind enough to include my work in the series. I thank him most sincerely, both for his confidence in me and for his unstinting advice; my thanks, too, to Janet Turner, Linda Kee and Priscilla Darrell whose remarks and suggestions enabled me to improve the structure and content.

I extend my deep appreciation to Mrs. Dorothy Crelinsten, who, besides translating this monograph, made many helpful suggestions throughout the editing process. I feel I owe her a great deal as "interpreter" of my work for my English-speaking readers. Finally, I would like to thank Mademoiselle Nicole Pinsonneault, who, with patience and precision, typed this text, reworking it a number of times as Mrs. Crelinsten and I made changes and additions. My many thanks to Professor André Normandeau, Director of the International Centre for Comparative Criminology, and to all my colleagues who gave me their support and facilitated the writing of this work. I trust it will make a positive contribution to the subject and bring new insight concerning the living conditions and apprehensions of the elderly.

The translation of this book was made under the auspices of the International Centre for Comparative Criminology of the University of Montreal with a grant from the research division of the Solicitor General of Canada.

Yves Brillon, Ph.D.
International Centre for
Comparative Criminology
University of Montreal

CONTENTS

TABLES

CHAPTER 1

CRIME, VIOLENCE AND THE ELDERLY

Largely because of the justice system's failure to fight crime, the fear of crime seems to be becoming more and more widespread. In Canada, the Canadian Urban Victimization Survey (Solicitor General 1984) shows that more than half the crimes committed (58%) are unknown to the police and 3% are known only because the police were actually present. This inability to effectively fight crime engenders apprehension and where the fear of crime is concerned, it creates a vicious circle, well described by Conklin (1981). He sums up the consequences of this rising fear as follows: feelings of insecurity and suspicion in a community will reduce the number of people on the street; this will have a direct effect on business, and an indirect effect as far as unemployment and the economic development of the region is concerned. With fewer people about, the streets become fairly deserted and hence more dangerous as unofficial social control becomes weakened. People who venture out become more vulnerable and therefore more frightened.

In Canada, a general fear of crime is true of a fairly high percentage of the urban population. Forty percent of a Canadian sample said they did not feel safe at night in their neighbourhood (Solicitor General of Canada 1983). According to this study, their fear is due to the fact that the public generally associates crime with violence. However, the fact is that, for Canadians, it is rarely violent. Canadians, as in all countries, are much more apt to be victims of crimes against property than personal attack. The authors of the study add:

> This is not to suggest that the experience of victimization is therefore typically a painless one with little lasting effect. A good deal of research, for example, has shown that many of the victims of break and enter, in particular, experience some form of crisis reaction quite apart from the suffering caused by their actual material loss. This invasion of one's home often produces a heightened concern about and fear of crime more generally (Solicitor General of Canada 1983, 2-3).

Crime engenders fear and has profound personal implications. It must not be forgotten that crime is frequently exaggerated by the mass media and exploited by certain groups, including the police forces, for partisan ends; it may be in their interest, by juggling figures and percentages, to show an

1

increased amount of crime, thus ensuring their power and prestige (Mohr, cited by Brown, 1976). Nor it is unusual in industrialized societies for the authorities, under the pretext of an apparent upsurge of violence, to demand more policemen, firearms and technological gadgets in order to take more punitive measures against violent criminals (Christie 1974).

It is obvious that, in a society where the fear of crime is clearly increasing, promises to reestablish law and order and make the streets safe once more are a good way of making sure of popular support (Conklin 1975). Under the pretext of reestablishing law and order, the authorities can take initiatives that, little by little, can lead to "punitive" solutions and repression[1].

THE IMPORTANCE OF STUDYING VICTIMIZATION AND FEAR OF CRIME AMONG THE ELDERLY

Almost every survey has shown that, although the rate of victimization is fairly low among senior citizens, it is they who most often show a fear of crime. The Canadian Urban Victimization Survey, in its conclusions (1985c), states that women are more apt to be fearful than men, persons 65 and over more than younger persons, victims of violent acts more than non-victims or than victims of crimes against property: "The group most likely to be fearful were elderly women who had recently been victimized, especially those who were victims of violent offences" (p. 3). It turns out, then, that elderly persons in general, and particularly women, are more fearful because they are especially vulnerable — or think they are. According to the authors of this Canadian study, the reason senior citizens are more fearful than others is because they feel that any criminal attack could have very serious consequences.

The study of victimization and fear of crime among the elderly is essential to understand certain important aspects that have a direct influence on the quality of their lives. It is all the more necessary in view of the very rapid increase in the number of aged persons in Canada, quite out of proportion to the rest of the population. The growing demographic weight of elderly persons is making the public at large aware of the often deplorable living conditions that characterize a fraction of this particular age group. Furthermore, surveys done in the United States and Canada have shown that fear of crime is a serious problem that many older persons have to face in their daily lives (Lecours and Roy 1982; Warr 1984). It is therefore imperative to analyze the attitudes of the elderly toward crime as well as the consequences it may have in the event that they become the victims of criminal attack.

THE IMPACT OF CRIME ON THE ELDERLY

The material, physical and psychological situation of the elderly have drawn the attention of the government and the public to the status of older Canadians. Along with this general awareness, criminology has initiated numerous victimization studies — a development that followed the publication of the results of the President's Commission on Law Enforcement and the Administration of Justice (1967). These have shown the vulnerability of the aged in a social milieu where violence and delinquency seem to be increasing and becoming more widespread.

Most of the studies from the United States, Europe and Canada on the effect of crime on the elderly seem to arrive at the same conclusions: Victimization, even if proportionately less frequent among older people than others, has psychological, material and physical consequences that are much more serious in their case than for the rest of the population (Alston 1986; Brillon 1986[2]; Solicitor General of Canada 1985; Lamarche and Brillon 1983). It is important to analyze not only the actual and objective victimization of elderly persons, but also their perceptions of the crime situation. This will tell us much about the consequences of crime — whether perceived or actually experienced — on their lives, their attitudes and their behaviour.

In this way we shall see, from their point of view, what crime means to the elderly, why they have such a fear of crime and fear of being victims of criminal attack. Specifically, this monograph seeks to answer the following questions: Feeling vulnerable, do old people tend to change their way of life? Do they resort to protective measures (alarm systems, locks and window bars, automatic light timers, guard dogs, firearms)? Are they forced to limit their outings (avoid certain city districts, not go out at night, use taxis because they are afraid of using public transportation, keep away from strangers, stay in the house, do their shopping only in the company of a friend or relative)? Are they forced into solitude and consequent feelings of apprehension (not answering the door or the telephone, being afraid of the neighbours, their surroundings)? Does the fear of crime, as many authors believe, result in the elderly "becoming prisoners in their own home"?

THE QUALITY OF LIFE AND FEAR OF CRIME AMONG THE ELDERLY

Ideas about crime and the fear of becoming victims of criminal attack are not concerns that can be analyzed in themselves without considering the social environment and the elderly persons' view of the world — the way they perceive others and society in general. Aging is a complex process that is as evident socially as it is individually, and the fear of crime seems to be connected with certain elements of this process. The Canadian Urban Victimization Survey (1985c) shows that the fact of being retired, of having lost one's mate or being alone are factors that contribute to the sense of vulnerability felt by the elderly. The reader may well ask, as do the authors of this study, whether being cut off from the normal activities of work and social contacts increases the feeling of vulnerability and, consequently, the fear of crime.

Obviously, the very living conditions that reduce the risk of victimization by keeping elderly persons away from potentially dangerous situations only increase the fear of crime. For example, "there is some indication that elderly people curtail their activities because of their fear of crime; they engage in far fewer evening activities than other age groups. At the same time, such withdrawal or isolation — whether a result of fear of crime or other factors associated with aging — may well aggravate the sense of vulnerability and fear felt by elderly people" (Solicitor General of Canada 1985c, 5). It is therefore essential that we understand the reasons for this fear of crime among the elderly so that policies can be adopted that will alleviate their apprehension and improve the quality of their lives.

In terms of the individual, age brings a greater risk of illness. The results of the Canada Health Survey of 1978–79, reported in the "Canadian Governmental Report on Aging" (1982) shows that among persons 65 and over, the number of sick days, the percentage of persons whose main activity is limited by some disability, and the proportion of those who suffer from ill-health is definitely higher than the national average. The highest figures are seen among those 75 years and over. Another fact that characterizes the elderly Canadian population and has a direct influence on the attitudes and behaviour of the women in particular, is the marked and increasing disparity between the number of men and women 65 and over. In 1980, the proportion was about 76 men for 100 women and, according to the estimates of the demography division (Statistics Canada 1979, no. 91–520), by the year 2000, there will be only 68 men for every 100 women.

These statistics show that among the elderly, there is a high proportion of single women with only a small income, who, because they are alone and defenceless, have a much greater fear of crime than men. Furthermore, half the women of 65 and over are widows, whereas less than a quarter of the men of this age group have lost their wives. Incidentally, the rate of marriages among widowers or divorcees is gradually increasing among men of advanced age whereas it is diminishing among the women. The proportion of women of 65 and over who live alone went from 15% in 1961 to 36% in 1981 (Chappell *et al.* 1986).

AGING AND ATTITUDES TOWARD CRIME

If there is a direct connection between age, victimization and the fear of crime it needs to be understood, because to a large extent it has yet to be defined in specific terms. It is certainly true that aging for many people means a slowing down of their activities; it limits their comings and goings and confines them more and more to their homes. The fact of going out less often obviously can lessen the degree of exposure to crime and therefore the rate of victimization. This may explain why the aged are generally less often the victims of crime than other age groups. According to Warr's observations (1984), when confronted with equal (apparent) chances of victimization, elderly people will still show greater fear than younger persons even if their perceived risk is lower. In Canada, we know that the probability of senior citizens living in urban areas being victims of violent crime is 12 times less than that of young people 16 to 24 years of age and 10 times less chance of being victims of a theft of personal property (Solicitor General of Canada 1985c). However, this does not tell us why the fear of Canadians 65 and over is so much greater than the risks involved in their case. There is apparently a complex association between the fear of crime and the living conditions of elderly persons. What needs to be established is to what degree the fear of crime combines with aging to restrict the activities of the aged and thus diminish the probability of their becoming victims. To do this, we must discover the connection between aging and fear, between fear in general and fear of crime specifically, and between the fear of crime and the lifestyle of the elderly. It is evident that growing old creates fears due to personal vulnerability — to accidents, sickness, solitude and poverty, for example. It seems that among old people, fear, victimization and vulnerability are experienced at two distinct levels, the one general and subjective (vague fear of crime, feeling of vulnerability and a general fear of facing life), the other concrete and objective (actually having been victimized; real fear engendered by crime; physical or psychic vulnerability due to a handicap or illness). All these elements stem, at least in part, from the conditions and style of life, and also act upon one another.

To come to a better understanding of the attitudes of the elderly toward crime, it is essential to define the particulars of their way of life, their way of thinking, their social integration, their world view, and their concerns and expectations. To understand the fear of crime among the elderly in such comprehensive terms calls for a combined approach, using the concepts, theories and methods of both criminology and gerontology.

AGEISM: SOCIETY'S REJECTION OF THE "OLD"

Several decades ago, Canada's birth rate dropped spectacularly, resulting in an increasing proportion of elderly people. Unfortunately, no consistent policies or programs were adopted to cope with this situation. Finally, the "old" were becoming an obvious problem, and if only because of their growing number, their deplorable living conditions and their isolation from the community, something had to be done about it. This problem required considerable human and financial resources.

In our industrialized and more and more automated societies, where what seems to count most are productivity, creativity, the future, competition, mobility, and speed and youth, we are beginning to see the covert emergence of a discriminatory attitude toward old people. This attitude, which gerontologists have termed "ageism", is a rejection of the elderly. As

McPherson (1983) explains: "Through the interaction of an age-stratification system and the socialization process, negative attitudes and stereotypes are formed and perpetuated so that the elderly are viewed as a distinct and unique group. Many of these views are reinforced by the media, in programs and advertisements emphasizing the high value placed on looking, thinking, feeling and acting young" (p. 251). Considering the ever-growing proportion of elderly persons in Canadian society, it would seem that the negative image of older people should gradually become less so. However, the fact remains that today, the attitude toward people in their 60s and over is too often negative and discriminatory, causing the more fragile to isolate themselves. The stronger, on the other hand, react more positively and will defend their rights, as in the case of the women in the United States who organized the "Grey Panthers" movement.

In this context, numerous authors extended the concept of victimization by including offences and acts not necessarily defined as criminal by the *Code*, but just as reprehensible (abuse, maltreatment, psychological suffering), and by adding the idea of "social victimization" to that of criminal victimization. This view is based on the fact that a certain proportion of the elderly population is exposed to negligence, discrimination, harassment and exclusion from all social life, situations against which, in many cases, they have no legal recourse. Taken to the extreme, aging becomes a process of victimization in itself (Reiman 1976; Rifai and Ames 1977). To paraphrase McDaniel (1986, 51), believing that aging can affect people negatively, some may develop a fear of aging, and even of old people. Without going that far, but taking into consideration the abuse and maltreatment of old people, the concept of victimization should be broadened beyond its strictly criminological definition in order to include behaviour that, without being criminal in itself, nonetheless has disastrous consequences for persons who are potentially vulnerable and defenceless.

We must be aware, too, that society, as well as governments, sometimes develop negative attitudes toward the elderly and are, therefore, responsible for the quality of their lives. As Powell (1980) says, sometimes governments in a way encourage the victimization of the aged. The fact that some housing projects for retired persons are built in poor districts, where the rate of crime is high, increases the risk of their becoming victims. More indirectly, the fact that old age pensions do not keep up with the cost of living increasing poverty among some, forces old people to live in high crime rate neighbourhoods or in inadequate housing. Old age has long been considered a time of rest and peace, of tranquillity and serenity. However, today, too often some older people are reduced to living a useless existence, at the same time knowing they are a burden to their families and to society. Policies and programs are therefore needed to integrate the elderly into a safe social environment, and to provide more meaning to their lives.

In this monograph, the term "elderly" refers to people 60 and over. This "statistical" definition varies, some researchers choosing the age of 65 and over, and some 60 and over. Therefore, it must be kept in mind that although chronological age is inescapable and depends on physiological factors, the same is not true of aging. The latter, while due to the biological process common to every living being, has both a social and individual element. As Massé and Brault (1984) noted, the elderly include recently retired persons of 60, 65 or 70, workers of all ages worn out by hard work, people happy to finally enjoy a life free from the constraints of a daily job, people of 75 and more who may be called old, but whose health, psychic functioning and degree of autonomy is far from being anything like the stereotyped image of "old age".

We would not want our readers to think from our analysis that the elderly form a homogeneous group of people who are all vulnerable, defenseless, ailing, isolated, poor and not sufficiently integrated in society. Our intention, rather, is to draw the attention of all those who deal with the elderly to a factor that alters the quality of life for many of them, namely, victimization and the fear it engenders. It is important that people be made aware of the problem so that action can be taken to improve the situation.

NOTES

1. We wanted to make the above comments before discussing crime and victimization among the elderly, for they are a target group that easily offers an opening for emotionalism. This threatens to distract certain researchers from their objective approach and to cause irrational reactions among the public.
2. This research was completed thanks to a grant from the Social Sciences and Humanities Research Council of Canada, Strategic Grants Program. A questionnaire was administered to a sample of 210 persons 60 years of age and over from the city of Montreal. The population comprises 96 men (46%) and 113 women (54%). The survey was conducted by means of personal interviews by the Centre de Sondage of the Université de Montréal during the Fall of 1983.

CHAPTER 2

THE VULNERABILITY OF THE ELDERLY VIS-À-VIS CRIME

Victimological research has shown that there is a close connection between people's *"style of life"*, their exposure to victimogenic situations (frequenting bars, night life, ostentatious display of certain possessions, etc.) and the degree of victimization. Generally speaking, it is young people between 18 and 25 who are most frequently the victims of crime, particularly violent crime. Compared with young people, the elderly, as we will see, are much less often victimized. The question is whether or not this is due to the fact that they prudently expose themselves less to potential danger — particularly any situation that would leave them open to criminal attack.

VULNERABILITY, VICTIMIZATION AND FEAR OF CRIME

Although the elderly are not the most victimized group in our society, nonetheless, they are among the most vulnerable. For people 65 and over in Canada, many elements of their living conditions explain this paradox, and can lead to a better understanding of their specific victimization. Their health situation, financial resources, housing and social integration have led many authors (Leother 1975; Hahn, Dussich, Lichman 1976; Logan, Ward 1979; Warr 1984) to speak of a greater vulnerability to crime where old people are concerned. This may seem to contradict the findings of victimization surveys which show that, with regard to most crimes, the victimization of elderly persons is proportionately much lower than that of other age groups.

The Canadian Urban Victimization Survey (1985c), for example, shows that, for all crimes, the rate of victimization varies significantly with age. Young people between the ages of 16 and 29 have a much greater probability of being victims than adults between 30 and 59, who, in turn, are more likely to be victims than persons 60 and over (see Table 2.1).

As Table 2.1 shows, 56% of the incidents of victimization (for 1981) involved the 16–29 age group; 39% of the crimes were committed against the 39–59 years olds and only 5% were aimed at persons 60 and over. These statistics have meaning only when compared with the distribution, in percentages, of these same age groups within the total Canadian population.

TABLE 2.1

**DISTRIBUTION, IN PERCENTAGES, OF DIFFERENT TYPES OF CRIME
ACCORDING TO AGE GROUP**

Types of crime	16 to 29	30 to 59	60 and over	Total
Sexual Assault	77%	21%	2%	100%
Robbery	66%	27%	7%	100%
Assault	71%	27%	2%	100%
Break and enter	44%	48%	8%	100%
Personal theft	52%	43%	5%	100%
Household theft	63%	34%	3%	100%
Vandalism	48%	46%	6%	100%
Totals	56%	39%	5%	100%

NOTE: The data used in this Table were compiled and organized from statistics furnished in November 1984 by the Department of the Solicitor General of Canada. I, alone, am responsible for the interpretation of these data.

This comparison appears in Table 2.2, based on the data of the 1981 census (Statistics Canada 1982).

The Canadian demographic statistics for 1981 show that persons 60 and over make up 14% of the total population. For purposes of comparison with the data of the Canadian Urban Victimization Survey, which concerned only citizens of 16 and over, we must know the proportion of citizens 60 and over contained in this group. The data of the census compiled in Table 2.2 show that persons from 15 to 29 represented 36% of all citizens over 15; those from 30 to 59 represented 46% of this population, and persons of 60 and over 18%. We can now compare these results with the distribution of incidents of victimization (Table 2.1). We find that the 16 to 29 group is disproportionately victimized with 56% of all offences, whereas it constitutes only 36% of the population surveyed; that the 30 to 59 group is less victimized (39% of all crimes for 46% of the population), and persons 60 and over are very seldom victimized (5% of incidents for 18% of the population surveyed).

Furthermore, elderly people are largely under-victimized, proportionately, for all types of crime. In descending order, they are: sexual assault (2% of crimes for 18% of the population, or an under-victimization of 16%); assault (−14%); household theft (−15%); personal theft (−13%); vandalism (−12%); robbery (−11%) and break and enter (−10%). For persons from 30 to 59 years of age, there is a balance between their demographic numbers and their victimization regarding break and enter (+2%), vandalism and personal theft (+3%). On the other hand, there is also a marked under-victimization regarding household theft (−12%); robbery and assault (−19%), and sexual assault (−25%). In the case of young people

TABLE 2.2

DISTRIBUTION OF THE CANADIAN POPULATION IN 1981, FOR FOUR AGE GROUPS

Age group	No. of inhabitants	% of the total population	% of the population 15 years of age and over
14 and under	5 481 105	22	—
15–29	6 836 305	28	36
30–59	8 685 475	36	46
60 and over	3 340 295	14	18
Totals	24 383 180	100	100

NOTE: These statistics were compiled from the data of the 1981 Census of Canada. Statistics Canada (1982).

(16–29), they are over-victimized with regard to every type of crime, particularly crimes of violence such as sexual assault (+41%); assault (+35%); and robbery (+30%). For crimes against property, the over victimization is less marked, although still proportionately high: household theft (+27%), personal theft (+16%), vandalism (+12%) and break and enter (+8%).

Most earlier studies confirm these results. Already in 1977, Hindelang *et al.* established the fact that people were victims of violence more often away from home than in the house or the immediate surroundings. It seems, then, as Cusson observes (1986), that the home has a protective function. People who spend more time than others away from home, either because of their age or their status, are more often victims of crime. According to studies from the time of Hindelang *et al.* (1978) to the Canadian Urban Victimization Survey (1985c), it appears that young people are more often the victims of crime than older people, workers more than retired or unemployed people and single people more than married people.

It is certain that lifestyles and "routine activities" influence the commission of crimes. Cusson (1986) and Felson and Cohen (1980) seem to offer parameters capable of enriching the victimological approach. They prompt us to question why — despite their vulnerability — elderly people are under-victimized, and to such a great extent. To answer this question, we must first describe certain characteristics of the elderly in order to better understand why they are not easy targets for potential criminals. We therefore analyse their "vulnerability" in terms of their state of health, their financial situation and their social milieu.

STATE OF HEALTH

As Chappell *et al.* (1986) note, we often evaluate a person's state of health in terms of chronic conditions, such as heart and circulation problems, arthri-

tis or rheumatism, palsy, failing eyesight, hearing problems, dental problems, stomach troubles and diabetes. People 65 and over suffer much more
from chronic illnesses (85.6%) than younger people (51.3%). In Canada, as
in the United States, the principal cause of death for the elderly is heart
disease, followed by cancer and then cerebral vascular disease. But these are
not necessarily the most frequent: "The most frequent chronic conditions
are heart disease, arthritis and chronic rheumatism, then hypertension; ...
the illnesses of old age are not necessarily the causes of mortality" (Chappell
et al. 1986, 35). Chronic deseases, however, must not be confused with
functional disabilities.

It is quite possible that illness is a source of anxiety and consequently can
have an effect on the fear of crime. We shall return to this subject in Chapter
5. Illness means fewer outings, especially alone, thus constituting an element of less exposure to the risk of victimization. The 1978–79 Canada
Health Survey (Health and Welfare Canada and Statistics Canada 1981)
shows that among people 65 and over, there are at least three times (35%)
the number who are handicapped in their daily life than among young persons (10%). Among the former, major activities are limited for 26% (house-
keeping, transportation, etc.) and 9% cannot do these things on their own.
This clearly shows that the ability to function for some tasks does decline
with age. But, some functions decline at different rates within the same individual.

In fact, both the number of chronic conditions and the extent of functional disability tend to increase with age. However, as Chappell *et al.*
(1986) point out, chronic conditions do not necessarily mean functional disability: "That is, while three-quarters of elderly persons have at least one
chronic condition, only about half experience some functional disability.
Even fewer, about one-fifth, require assistance with basic activities" (p. 37).
The fact remains that this means 20% to 25% of elderly citizens in Canada
are seriously limited in their movements and activities, which can mean less
exposure to criminal victimization. It can also mean, however, as we shall
see in Chapter 5, a greater probability of neglect, abuse and maltreatment.

Aging, because it is accompanied by a loss of strength and physical resistance, increases people's vulnerability. Skogan and Maxfield (1981) define
physical vulnerability as "openness" to aggression, an inability to defend
oneself against an assailant and the possibility of being exposed during an
attack to physical (and probably emotional) trauma. An older person,
because of his often weakened physical condition, becomes less alert, and
less quick to react. Moreover, older people may look weak and defenceless,
and thus become an easy prey to a potential aggressor. To illustrate, a
study, in which 40 elderly persons in Montreal were interviewed (Lamarche
and Brillon 1983), confirms that the very appearance of the aged invites
attack: "even visually, the fact of having hunched shoulders and walking
slowly can make one a potential victim" (p. 35). It is not only bodily

appearance that makes the elderly person an easy target: "By his manner, the way he clutches his wallet, the way he looks about suspiciously, will attract an attack" (id. p. 35), most often by youths on the lookout for a helpless victim.

It is precisely because their assailants in most cases are men, and mostly young men, that elderly people are unable to defend themselves. Their image of the criminal, therefore, is "a young hoodlum" who is a constant threat, whereby all young people become potential criminals, not to be trusted. It is perhaps this perception of crime as a direct threat that becomes generalized for the aged and differentiates them from the rest of the population, who see the criminal in a more general or less threatening way. This was the finding of the qualitive study cited above (Lamarche and Brillon 1983). A social worker, working with elderly persons, aptly summed up this aspect of the classic conflict between the generations: "The elderly identify the fear of victimization with young criminals. They then extend this fear to the point where all young people, in their eyes, become more or less future criminals" (p. 34).

According to research findings, when the aged are attacked there is a greater chance of their being injured, and seriously so. For example, 25.5% of young victims of an offence sustain injuries and of these, 19.7% must be hospitalized. In contrast, for victims 65 and over the percentages are 41.9% and 27.5%, respectively (Conklin 1976). It is important that this physical impact be taken into account, as well as the psychological consequences of victimization among the elderly.

THE FINANCIAL SITUATION

With advancing age, there is most often a reduction in financial resources. Having only a small income — their old age pension — a number of persons 65 and over live in a state of great financial insecurity. In Canada, in 1982, 70% of families headed by an elderly person had an income of $25,000 and less as opposed to 27% of families headed by persons from 45 to 54 years of age. A large percentage of older families — four out of ten — had an income even lower than $15,000. Among unattached persons, 72% of persons 65 and over had an income of $10,000 and less as opposed to 28% among persons from 35 to 44 (National Council of Welfare: *Sixty-Five and Older*, 1984). According to this study, the situation of elderly women was infinitely worse than that of men. In fact, in 1982, the great majority of women 65 and over had incomes under $10,000 compared to 54% of elderly men.

It must be said, however, that in the last few years the financial situation of elderly persons has somewhat improved. Statistics[1] from 1984 show that 11.4% of elderly families were considered to have a low income, compared with 21.9% in 1979. For unattached persons, 49.6% of elderly people had a low income in 1984 as opposed to 66.3% in 1979. Although there are fewer poor than before among elderly persons in Canada, the fact remains that it is this group that has the largest proportion of persons living on a low income.

The National Council of Welfare (1984) states that most elderly Canadians have modest incomes and that a large number of citizens 65 and over live below the poverty level. This study shows that government social security programs and pensions provide almost all (more than 75%) of the incomes of senior citizens in the low income category. It is evident that most people who are poor or borderline cases before the age of 65 will remain poor during their old age. What is less evident is that many Canadians with average incomes become poor or live on a low income after they retire. The study, *Sixty-Five and Older* (1984) estimates that public programs for elderly persons replace hardly more than half of the income a single person had before retiring. This, incidentally, corresponds to the American data. According to Rifai and Ames (1977), the average income of retired persons in the United States is about half the salary they earned when they were working. Thus, in Canada, according to the 1984 study, two-thirds of Canadians with average incomes must face a reduction of 25% or more in income after retirement. As we have seen, women are the most affected by this age-related impoverishment.

This relative poverty among people over 65, especially women, has a direct influence on their way of life. Some frequently live in inadequate lodgings, for instance. In Canada, in 1982, 75% of senior families and 40% of seniors living alone owned their own place of residence. Among them, there were as many with low incomes as those who were more affluent. Consequently, with the high cost of maintaining a home, the former found themselves in financial difficulty. Their chief asset provided a roof over their heads, but at the same time took a large portion of their modest incomes. For elderly home-owners, unexpected expenses are a source of much anxiety and often force them to do without other esentials. It must be remembered that their homes are generally old and require frequent and sometimes costly repairs (National Council of Welfare 1984). The financial situation of elderly citizens is rather precarious, and, as we shall see, generates a "general fear" of the future, which in turn can have a bearing on the fear of crime.

The Montreal survey (Brillon 1986) of 210 persons of 60 and over shows that it is among the most elderly age group that we find the poorest senior citizens and those who live in the poorest neighbourhoods. A majority of persons between 60 and 65 (64%) lived in areas where there is a low rate of crime, whereas a majority of persons 75 and over (62%) were for the most part concentrated in crime-ridden districts. The same study clearly shows that income is the foremost determining factor in terms of both the housing conditions and residential stability of elderly people. Because of a strong correlation between income and age and between sex and marital status, women and single persons 65 and over experience the worst housing conditions and change residences most frequently. When we say that many senior citizens do not have adequate living conditions, we refer not only to the lodgings, but the neighbourhood as well. Logan (1979) made a connection between revenue and neighbourhood when she spoke of "limited choices as the result of limited incomes". She deplores this situation, stating that:

> Available housing for low-or-fixed income elderly is often severely restricted to older, deteriorating buildings in dying neighbourhoods or high rises imposing a monastic isolation by their distance from bus lines and centers of activity (1979, 129–130).

The modest incomes of a majority of persons 65 and over, incomes that have become insufficient after the age of retirement, have forced them to live in more or less poor neighbourhoods. With the years, many of these neighbourhoods have become run-down and unsafe, but due to a lack of means, many elderly persons are unable to move to healthier and safer areas. A number of authors (Nelson *et al.* 1975; Cunningham 1976; Wolfe 1977) acknowledge the fact that it is because of their low incomes that there are so many senior citizens living in crime-ridden districts.

Unlike wealthier citizens who have left such areas for new and safer neighbourhoods, those on low, fixed incomes must remain. The general deterioration and high rate of crime in these areas can be a source of fear for the elderly, who consequently tend to confine themselves to their homes. They go out less, thus avoiding the risk of being attacked or robbed. In short, the greater vulnerability of senior citizens is the very reason for their lower rate of victimization.

In Canada, in 1961, 12% of elderly persons (10% of the men and 15% of the women) were living alone compared to 24% (14% of the men and 36% of the women) in 1981 (Chappell *et al.* 1986). According to the National Council of Welfare (1984), this substantial increase, the number of senior citizens living alone having doubled in 20 years, represents a major change in Canadian society. This is explained by the fact that although most men and women are married when they reach 65, many more women have to face widowhood than vice versa. They generally live longer than their husbands, who are usually the older of the two. In 1981, according to the data of the National Council of Welfare, six elderly women out of ten were without a husband, in most cases, widowed. Among elderly men, on the other hand, three out of four were married, and only 14% had lost their wives.

Some of the principal factors that characterize the way of life and social environment of the elderly in Canada clearly show their vulnerability. Ten percent of the families and almost half the persons living alone have a low income; nearly a quarter of all senior citizens live alone and 35% suffer from an illness that more or less severely limits their ability to accomplish daily tasks and other activities. One of the factors that seems more specific perhaps to this age group is the considerable difference between the living conditions of the men and those of the women.

Growing old for a woman means financial hardship, loneliness and illness far more than it does for a man. Living a long time, for some women, unfortunately, is synonymous with a life of anxiety due to developments that they often find very difficult to cope with. When this anxiety and vulnerability occur, do they play a role in the elderly person's perception of crime and the fear of becoming a victim? We shall come back to this question in order to explain the various forms of fear that the elderly have concerning crime.

The aging process is accompanied in varying degrees by illness or physical handicaps that make people more vulnerable in the sense that they are less able to defend themselves against a potential offender, and if attacked, are more apt to suffer serious consequences. This is also true for crimes against property. Since a proportionately greater number of senior citizens have low incomes, if robbed, they will suffer more hardship because of the loss than more affluent persons would. Furthermore, the Canadian Urban Victimization Survey (1985c) concludes that, when attacked, persons 65 and over were more apt to need medical care and, when robbed, they were more apt to suffer a greater loss in proportion to income than other age groups. Added to this are certain psychological factors connected with aging: "Older people may ... perceive less ability to cope with disruptive changes than younger people. They may, for example, feel that there is less time available to cope with change and replace what may have been lost" (Ward 1979, 124). As Warr says (1984), these factors are concomitants of the aging process and add to the greater physical vulnerability of old people.

It is important, then, to distinguish the potential "vulnerability" of the elderly from their probability of victimization. Age is accompanied by circumstances that make people more likely to be cheated or robbed (failing eyesight, for example, which makes it easy to short-change someone making a purchase). At the same time, however, for a number of old people, age is accompanied by changes in lifestyle (due perhaps to the loss of a mate, to retirement, a reduction in financial resources, the onset of chronic illness or a functional disability, etc.) whereby certain persons 65 and over are much less often exposed to the possibility of attack than younger people.

ELDERLY PEOPLE AS "SUITABLE TARGETS" FOR CRIME

Considering what has been said so far about the victimization and living conditions of the elderly, it would be interesting to know *what type of target* they represent for the criminal. For example, Felson and Cohen (1980) believe that "any successfully complete violation requires at a minimum an *offender* with both criminal inclination and the ability to carry out those inclinations, a person or object providing a *suitable target* for the offender, and the *absence of guardians* capable of preventing the violation. The lack of any of these elements is sufficient to prevent a potential direct-contact predatory violation from succeeding" (p. 392). In their study, based on the evolution of crime in the United States, the authors show that the absence of a guardian capable of protecting property is one of the most important conditions in the commission of a crime. It is when people leave their houses or apartments (to go to work, to study or for amusement) that criminals lying in wait have the best chance of success; all the more so if their target (whether an object or a person) has little protection or none at all. As Cusson (1986) says, it is much easier to protect oneself and one's property when one stays at home.

This being the case, since many elderly persons, generally go out less often than young people, they do not make "suitable targets". By staying in, they deter offenders from attacking them or their property. Thus, some factors of vulnerability (health, solitude, low income), because they confine certain people, are indirect elements of protection. Elderly people who live alone and go out very little are much more sheltered from danger than they may think. This is seen later when the fear of crime among people 60 and over is discussed. To this must be added the fact that 77% of elderly men and 47% of elderly women live with their spouses, and this reinforces the presence in the home and, at the same time, increases the protection of the persons themselves and their property. This partly explains why the victimization of older people is proportionately less than that of other age groups.

In a study some time ago, Reppeto (1974) showed that one of the principal fears of break and enter offenders was to find themselves face to face with their victim. Seventy percent of the criminals questioned said that the information they wanted most was whether or not the occupants were at home. This shows how effective a deterrent retirement can be for the elderly, since they no longer go to work and since they remain at home a great deal. The presence or absence of the occupants of a house is a prime consideration for house-breakers (Winchester and Jackson 1983).

It is on the street that elderly people become most vulnerable, especially since, compared with others, they are much less able to defend themselves. It follows, then, that women of 60 and over are even more vulnerable. According to Cusson (1986), the risk that a potential thief or aggressor runs is that much less if the victim is incapable of thwarting him, wounding him or killing him. Away from home, an elderly person, and particularly an elderly woman alone, becomes a much more suitable target for the potential offender. The basic premise of Hough, Clarke and Mayhew (1980) is very apt: "Criminal opportunities exist not only where the material conditions are present but where benefits can be gained at low risk" (p. 5). Older people, when alone in the street and defenceless, constitute a low risk for offenders. That is why they are primarily victims of petty theft, especially purse-snatching.

Criminal opportunities also depend largely on the accessibility of the target, geographically and socially. Research has shown that offenders prefer to act close to their homes and in neighbourhoods with which they are very familiar (Fréchette 1984; Maguire 1982). This geographic proximity is quite often neutralized by the fact that elderly persons, being more often at home, keep potential criminals at a distance, in a way. Socially, on the other hand, different lifestyles keep most older people apart from offenders: "Adolescents are three times more often victimized than older people because they go out more often and their way of life brings them in contact with potential criminals" (Cusson 1986, 64). Another reason why the elderly are less often victimized, then, would be largely because they make themselves less accessible.

OLD AGE AND THE FEELING OF BEING VULNERABLE

Many elderly people are aware of their weakness and vulnerability. The majority, more than anything else, are afraid of being personally attacked, although there is very little risk of their being victims of this type of crime. For example, research done in Montreal (Brillon 1986) shows that of the 210 persons 60 and over who were interviewed, 53% of the men and women were afraid of being burglarized in their absence; 69% of the women and 39% of the men feared being attacked in their home, and 69% of the women and 47% of the men feared being attacked away from home.

On the basis of their responses, there can be no doubt about how apprehensive these respondents feel about the physical consequences of an attack. What old people mainly fear is criminal assault. Of the 179 persons who, in the same survey, answered a question on the consequences of victimization they feared the most, 34% answered they were afraid of being crippled, 29% of being injured, 17% of being psychologically traumatized and 12% of being murdered.

Another indication of the vulnerability elderly people feel is the fact that they have the impression they can do nothing to prevent criminal attack. A Canadian survey[2] (Brillon *et al.* 1984) found that only 19% of people 60 and over thought they could do something, alone or with others, to reduce the crime in their neighbourhood. Among persons from 31 to 60, a third believed there were steps they could take to curb crime, and among those 30 and younger, almost half (49%) said they could do something, at the community level, to fight crime. This feeling of helplessness or resignation among the elderly has a direct influence on their fear of crime. Obviously, if they see crime as an inevitable evil, as something over which they have no control, then their only protection is avoidance or flight!

The Montreal study supports this hypothesis. The data clearly show that people 60 and over who become involved in the life of the community, in activities such as participation in leisure groups, arts and crafts or political gatherings, feel much safer in their neighbourhood than those who have no social activities. The relationship between active involvement and feeling secure is positive and significant[3]. By confining themselves to their apartments, old people increase their fear and their feelings of vulnerability, whereas those who remain active in community organizations maintain contact with the reality of their surroundings. They are therefore better able to evaluate the real dangers in the area, uninfluenced by exaggerated reports of the rate of crime and the risk of attack.

LEVELS OF PERCEPTION

Numerous authors (Biderman *et al.* 1967; Garofalo 1977; Figgie 1980; Group for Research on Attitudes toward Crime (G.R.A.C.) 1984) have shown that there are different levels of perception that form and develop people's images of crime and the criminal. First, there is the relatively abstract level where crime is perceived as a matter of serious concern. This feeling is based less on direct experience than on an impression, confirmed by the violence depicted by the media, that there is a rapid, even spectacular, increase in serious crime, especially crime against the person — crime that evokes an image of the most atrocious and terrifying acts.

Second, at the more concrete and immediate level, people more or less objectively and accurately evaluate the extent of the evolution of crime in their immediate area — in their neighbourhood, for instance. Thus it seems that the closer we get to actual experience and the daily reality as it exists, the less distorted and stereotyped the interpretation is of the crime situation. In fact, when it comes to their own neighbourhoods, people differentiate between what they perceive and the exaggerated accounts the newspapers are likely to present.

In the same way, researchers indicate that the less people know about the system of justice or the persons involved (judges, police, criminals, victims) and the less they are exposed to, or have experienced, victimization, the more they tend to generalize their image of the criminal, who then becomes the "dangerous criminal". This is most often an abstract image triggered by an emotional reaction to the consequences implied in the social images of crime. Hence, it is the question of people's perception of the evolution of crime and their image of the criminal that will be examined now.

CONCLUSION

Because of the aging process, certain factors make elderly persons more vulnerable to victimization than other age groups. In Canada, one in five individuals 65 and over have health problems that limit their activities; consequently, they are forced to stay home a great deal. This, undeniably, is a concrete factor that should explain why the elderly are less often the victims of crime than other age groups. However, on the other hand, it will be shown that illness and dependence can play a role in the development of negligence, abuse and ill treatment on the part of relatives, the personnel in institutions, or anyone who has to take care of old people suffering from a functional disability.

Regarding the financial factor, there are generally more older people with low incomes than other citizens. Among those 65 and over, one family in ten lives below the poverty level and, for persons living alone, the ratio is two out of ten. More women than men are poverty stricken, and almost twice as many live on insufficient incomes. Moreover, many senior citizens live in old neighbourhoods that have greatly deteriorated over the years, and which, in many cases, have a high rate of crime. In the following chapters, the relationship that may exist between the living conditions of the aged and their fear of crime will be discussed.

It is being acknowledged, more and more, that although the elderly are victims of crime less often than younger people, victimization when it occurs is more distressing, harder to bear and more devastating. Because there are more old people, proportionately, who are vulnerable psychologically, physically and financially, it is easy to understand that, for them, a theft, an attack or ill treatment can have more serious consequences than for younger persons in better health and in better financial circumstances. Ward (1979), for example, believes that a loss of property "may be more subjectively threatening for older than for younger people. Their loss represents a greater destruction of time and symbolic assets" (p. 124). If this is so for attacks on property, one can imagine how much more serious the consequences of personal attack would be. It all depends, of course, on the psychic and physical "vulnerability" of the elderly person, which is not only a matter of age, but many other circumstances.

NOTES

1. Statistics compiled and organized by Professor Cope Schwenger, University of Toronto: Program in gerontology.
2. This research was requested and financed by the Department of the Solicitor General of Canada. The "theoretical" sample was made up of a largely urban population (Montreal, Toronto and Winnipeg: (614 persons) and a rural population from the provinces of Quebec, Ontario and Manitoba (203 persons). The total sample comprises 817 subjects. For further detail, see Brillon, Louis-Guérin and Lamarche (1984). The remarks made here are solely those of the author. The survey took place in 1981.
3. Gamma = .33; p = .004

CHAPTER 3

PERCEPTION OF CRIME AMONG THE ELDERLY

People, regardless of age, generally tend to perceive crime as being on the increase at the national level much more so than in the area in which they live (Garofalo 1977). Therefore, they evaluate the rate of crime as being much higher "elsewhere" than in their own neighbourhood (Biderman *et al.* 1967; Boggs 1971). Furstenberg Jr. (1972) was one of the first to have made a distinction between general concern about crime and a specific evaluation of the risk of victimization. General concern, he feels, is due to a value judgment as to the importance of crime in relation to other social problems, whereas evaluation of the risks involved is due to a fear of crime.

Fowler and Mangione (1974) have contributed a subtler conceptual nuance by making a distinction between an evaluation of the risks and an emotional reaction to the threat of crime. People can make the same assessment of their risk of victimization, but react differently when threatened, depending on the extent of their anxiety. These distinctions are important for, in terms of the individual, they will not have the same influence on behaviour and attitudes, particularly when it comes to the divergent perceptions of different age groups.

THE RELATIVE IMPORTANCE OF CRIME

The importance given to crime in comparison with other social problems reflects a moral conception of what is not acceptable — what is to be tolerated or not in a given community. Among certain individuals or groups, however, the pre-eminence of crime compared with other social problems also depends on their perception of the rates of crime as well as their economic and social situation, the visibility of certain dramatic events (spectacular or contemptible crimes, such as the murder of old people) and the urgency of other individual or community problems. Therefore, we have a very incomplete picture of people's concern about crime in their daily life. Even though in the past 15 years or so there seems to be more and more general anxiety among the public, crime being considered one of the two or three most serious problems in society (Biderman *et al.* 1972; Erskine 1974; Stinchcombe *et al.* 1980; Figgie Report 1980), it is possible that this aspect has only a very indirect effect on people's fear and the precautions they take.

During a national survey of 817 Canadians conducted by the Group for Research on Attitudes toward Crime (G.R.A.C.) of the Université de Montréal, and with the aid of person-to-person interviews, each respondent was asked to indicate what in his opinion were the most important social problems in Canadian society. For 32%, the economy (inflation, unemployment) proved to be the most important; for 19.2%, it was crime; for 18.8% values and for 14.1%, inequalities and social injustice.

With regard to the persons who feel that crime is the principal social problem, the data indicate that their number increases with age. More than 11% (11.4%) are young people of 30 or under, 22% range from 31 to 59 and 24.2% are 60 years of age and over. Among the latter, the proportion varies according to sex — 16.5% of the men versus 30.1% for the women. This proportion also fluctuates according to geographical location. Eighteen percent of older people living in a rural area — our rural sample was taken from the provinces of Quebec (N = 81), Ontario (N = 57) and Manitoba (N = 66) — consider the crime problem a matter of priority as against 26% of those living in Montreal (N = 222), Toronto (N = 254) and Winnipeg (N = 138).

THE INFLUENCE OF PROXIMITY ON THE PERCEPTION OF CRIME

On a relatively abstract level, it is mostly the elderly who see crime as a serious national problem. This feeling seems to be based less on immediate knowledge than an impression, confirmed by the violence depicted by the mass media, of a rapid increase in "serious crime", that is, violent crime. This perception is largely due to fear of the unknown. The more events are impossible to control, the more threatening they become.

The following table 3.1 shows that for all age groups, the rate of crime is perceived to be higher when the area concerned is far away and unfamiliar. In the Canadian sample (G.R.A.C. 1984), 74% of those surveyed thought the national rate had increased a great deal; 57% (17% less) believed this was the case in their city or village and only 37% (half that at the national level) were of the opinion that crime had greatly increased in the vicinity in which they lived. We find that the estimation of a marked increase in crime, whether at the national, local or neighbourhood level, is directly related to age. Almost all the respondents of 60 and over (91%) believe that the crime rate in Canada has definitely increased over the past five years against 62% of those of 30 and under, while 61% of elderly persons against 52% of the youngest groups think this is true of their city or village. The gap between the age groups lessens when they refer to their place of residence. Regarding their neighbourhood, there is only a difference of 7% between those 30 and under (35%) and those 65 and over (42%).

These data indicate a general tendency to over-estimate the volume of crime when one is likely to be apprehensive, as is often the case for older

TABLE 3.1

PERCEPTIONS ABOUT CRIME RATES ACCORDING TO PROXIMITY, FOR THREE AGE GROUPS (1981)

	Number of respondents (N) in each age group in the sample (S) who agree that the rate of crime has greatly increased, in:					
	Canada		My locality		My neighbourhood	
Age group	N/S**	%	N/S	%	N/S*	%
39 and under	147/237	62	122/237	52	69/196	35
31 to 59	290/398	73	236/398	59	124/339	37
60 and over	166/182	91	111/182	61	51/120	42
Totals	603/817	74	469/817	57	244/655	37

NOTE: Survey done in 1981 in the cities of Winnipeg, Toronto and Montreal and in rural areas of Manitoba, Ontario and Quebec (G.R.A.C., N = 817).

 * In the rural areas where neighbourhoods have no geographical identity, only 655 of the sample responded instead of 817.

** The numbers indicate the answers given, in each category, for all respondents in that category.

people. The same tendency is also found where the risk of victimization is concerned. The fact remains, however, that there is a distinct difference between perceptions of crime at the national and local levels; hence, caution is necessary when we speak of the impact of crime on people's lives and of their growing anxiety in the face of what they see as an increase in crime. We must differentiate here between the two levels of perception, for they do not have the same influence on people's behaviour.

Some American studies have already shown this tendency to perceive a much greater increase at the national than at the local level (Garofalo 1977). The difference can be explained by the relatively abstract nature of national estimates, which are generally determined by public discourse — usually alarmist. Local estimates, on the other hand, are based more on signs within the surrounding area and on daily experience, resulting in a more realistic estimate of the immediate crime situation. Another element that often colours these evaluations is the tendency to think that crime is always more serious and more alarming elsewhere than in one's own immediate and more familiar vicinity. The fact is that most people fear the unknown; the less familiar someone is with a place and the people there, the more suspicious he is. A study done about ten years ago showed a significant relationship between the fear of crime and suspicion of strangers (President's Commission 1967).

The study by G.R.A.C. (Brillon *et al.* 1984) shows that when judging the crime situation in Canada as a whole, people have few concrete signs to judge by and can only make an evaluation that is most often based on media reports. The information gleaned in this way is second-hand and there is no concrete point of reference. But, as soon as the ground is more familiar, perceptions can be based on signs in the immediate environment (activities of the police, number of crimes; vandalism, activities of the youth, acquaintances who have been victims of attack, etc.) and daily experience. People know their own district and can therefore more accurately judge the evolution and nature of the crime in their neighbourhood and the specific risks involved.

CRIME AS A DAILY CONCERN

We have seen that elderly persons are more aware of crime as a social problem than younger people. A greater number of them, proportionately, consider it one of the main problems of society and perceive it as increasing rapidly. The importance given crime, however, is relative when the daily concerns of the aged are considered. In a Montreal survey of 210 persons of 60 and over (Brillon, Cousineau and Gravel 1983), respondents were asked to state the problem that concerned them most in their daily lives. Of the 210 persons questioned, 64 (30.5%) said they had no particular problems and two did not answer at all. Among the 144 who did answer, the problems in order of importance were as follows:

44%: Problems of a physical nature or a matter of health (aging, illness, hospitalization, etc.).
21%: Problems of a psychological nature (insecurity, frustration, fear of retirement, solitude, etc.)
14%: Financial problems (money, unemployment, cost of living, inflation, housing, etc.)
13%: Problems concerning the children and family unity (the future, family, education, drugs, etc.)
4%: Crime, delinquency (violence, drugs, etc.)
4%: Other

It may seem paradoxical that crime ranks fifth in the list of personal concerns of a population in which, as discussed further on, the fear of crime plays such an important role that it limits the movements of its members. This is due to the fact that the questionnaire specified that the respondent give "only one answer" regarding "the problem that concerns you most in your daily life". It is evident that, for the elderly, physical and psychological health, income and the family situation are of vital importance and rank higher than the problem of crime. This is because these problems are inevitable. There is no way to escape aging, illness, or the death of a husband or wife (which will probably entail a reduction in income, especially for women). Crime is frightening, but it seems possible to avoid it, if only at the expense of a great deal of freedom of action. This study supports similar American studies. For example, in order to find out whether crime was a problem that affected older people, Ragan (1977) assessed the perception of crime as a problem among a community of Blacks, Mexicans and Whites between 54 and 74 years of age. She concluded that, generally speaking, older people did not consider crime a major problem. Only 5% to 36% of the people studied, depending on the group, saw crime as a priority concern.

When the questionnaire offers multiple choice, crime and the fear of crime have a higher rating in relation to other concerns of the elderly. In 1975, Harris compared the general public's view of the problems specific to the elderly with that expressed by persons 65 and over. His findings show that whereas 50% of the public acknowledged that the fear of crime was a very serious problem, only 47% of the elderly thought so. The difference in the results was due to the question of priorities. The public placed the fear of crime in fourth place after lack of money (62%), solitude (60%) and ill health (51%); whereas the elderly mentioned fear of crime second, after ill health (50%) and before financial difficulties (40%). Another study by Clarke and Lewis (1982) tends to show that the fear of personal victimization ranks third. Depending on location and the population studied, the methodology and type of research, the results generally lead to the same conclusion. All the studies place crime as one of the four or five principal concerns of the elderly.

THE IMAGE OF CRIME AND THE CRIMINAL

According to the Canadian survey already cited (G.R.A.C. 1984), the most frequent complaint of the majority of citizens is that magistrates are much too lenient in their sentencing. In fact, 72% of our survey sample felt that, generally speaking, the sentences handed down by the criminal courts were not severe enough. Doob and Roberts (1983), analyzing the results of a Gallup poll of a sample of 1,062 Canadians, arrive at an even higher percentage. According to their study, 80% of Canadians find the sentences imposed by the courts too mild or too lenient. These answers were found to be closely related to education: university-educated respondents were slightly less likely to think that sentences were not severe enough (74%) than the less educated (81%). The authors also discovered regional differences. The percentage of people believing "sentences are not severe enough" was 74.3% in the Atlantic provinces; 77.3% in Quebec; 78.6% in Ontario; 81.7% in the Prairies and 88.1% in British Columbia. Although the differences are not very great, they are nonetheless statistically significant.

The G.R.A.C. study found a strong positive correlation between age and a view that sentences imposed by judges are not severe enough. This is clearly shown in the table 3.2.

As the figures show, whereas 59% of those under 30 find the sentences not severe enough, 75% of people aged 31 to 60 and a very large majority of

TABLE 3.2

CANADIAN OPINIONS OF COURT SENTENCES FOR THREE AGE GROUPS (1981)

| | The sentences pronounced by the court are: | | | | | | | |
| Age group | Too severe | | Sufficiently severe | | Not severe enough | | Total subjects | |
	N	%	N	%	N	%	N	%
30 and under	22	9	75	31	140	59	237	29
31 to 59	10	3	89	22	299	75	398	49
60 and over	2	1	34	19	146	80	182	22
Totals	34	4	198	24	585	72	817	100
$r = 0.20$	$p = .0000$							

NOTE: Survey done in 1981 in the cities of Winnipeg, Toronto and Montreal and in rural areas of Manitoba, Ontario and Quebec (G.R.A.C., N = 817).

older people (80%) share this opinion. However, this opinion, although it expresses what Canadians think, does not convey "the whole truth". What these data seem to show is that there is a gap between the decisions of the courts and the severity of the punishments desired by the citizens. Such an analysis of the results of the surveys seems superficial, excessive and even fallacious — fallacious to the extent that it leads to the belief that the majority of citizens think that the majority of punishments imposed on the majority of criminals are not severe enough.

This assumption is entirely false, and yet it continues to be accepted. The reality is that when the citizens are asked whether, in general, they consider the sentences handed down by the courts "too severe", "just severe enough" or "not severe enough", most of them answer, not in terms of criminals in general, but with reference to the most dangerous criminals. This, in any case, is what emerges from a survey done by the Centre de Recherche sur l'Opinion Publique (C.R.O.P. 1980), one based on an analysis of a Gallup poll by Doob and Roberts (1983) and on our own survey (G.R.A.C. 1984).

In these three surveys, people were asked to specify the type of criminal they were thinking of when giving their opinion on the severity of sentences. In C.R.O.P.'s sample, 60% of the respondents were thinking of violent criminals (41% of murderers, 5% of rapists and 14% of dangerous criminals, those involved in armed robberies, grievous assault, kidnapping). Of the 70% of the public who said the sentences were not severe enough, 85%, or almost all of them, were referring to dangerous criminals. The same finding was derived from our own data. Of the 72% who thought judges were too lenient, 64% had hardened criminals in mind (murderers, assassins, rapists, etc.). Doob and Roberts (1983) observed that members of the public who think that sentences are too lenient (80%) have violence in mind when they express the opinion that sentences are not harsh enough. They found that about a third of the respondents had all criminals in mind, and that over half were thinking of either violent or persistent offenders. Furthermore, these same people — those who consider the criminal court sentencing too lenient — are the most likely to over-estimate the amount of violent crime in Canada. It seems obvious, then, that for the public, it is the dangerous criminal — the recidivist, the habitual criminal — who serves as the yardstick by which it judges the severity of the courts. The fact is that in Canada, only 8% of all criminals fall into this category.

Again, it is the elderly who have the most negative and most frightening image of the criminal. More than younger people, they see offenders as murderers (38% of those 60 and over and 26% of those 30 and under) or as violent individuals (28% *vs.* 18%). Table 3.3 shows that the criminal they really fear is a violent person, extremely formidable because of the serious crimes he commits.

TABLE 3.3

PERCEPTION OF THE CRIMINAL AS A DANGEROUS INDIVIDUAL FOR THREE AGE GROUPS (1981)

					Violent persons		Total respondents	
What type of criminal have you in mind when judging the severity of the courts?								
	Murderers		Rapists					
Age group	N	%	N	%	N	%	N	%
30 and under	60	26	22	10	40	18	122/226	54
31 to 59	122	33	41	11	81	22	244/369	66
60 and over	64	38	12	7	46	28	122/167	73
Totals	246	32	75	10	167	22	488/762	64

Corrélation between age and number of respondents having a dangerous criminal in mind: gamma = .17; p = .001

NOTE: Survey done in 1981 in the cities of Winnipeg, Toronto and Montreal as well as in rural areas of Manitoba, Ontario and Quebec (G.R.A.C., N = 817).

It is evident, according to these statistics, that a person's image of the criminal is closely connected with age. Among the 30-year-olds and under, a little more than half (54%) of those questioned think of dangerous individuals when they think of criminals. This proportion rises to 66% among the 31 to 59-year-olds, and to 73% among those 60 and over. Yet, as we have pointed out, the idea in people's minds that most criminals are violent in no way corresponds with the facts. This gap between the reality and the perception of the criminal seems to be due to the fact that the population's opinion of crime and the criminal justice system is based on information that conveys only part of the picture.

Doob and Roberts, who studied this problem give the following reasons for the ignorance of the public:

> First, exceptional, dramatic cases ... are both vivid and salient, two dimensions that are known to enhance recall and to affect subjects' judgments. Second, people tend to seek confirming rather than disconfirming [sic] instances. Thus if a person believes the courts are overly-lenient, he or she will seek, when asked, sentences which support the attitude rather than those which do not support it. Finally, there is also evidence that important social attitudes, of which judicial leniency is surely one, guide our memories of relevant information. Thus, if a person believes the courts are too lenient, he is more likely to remember sentences that were lenient rather than ones that were harsh (Doob and Roberts 1983, 2).

The citizens are rarely fully informed about crime and the criminal justice system. Instead of the Department of Justice giving them a broader view, their main sources of information are the "media", which tend to project a distorted image of the crime situation. What they usually report are the small number of violent acts that make the front page of the newspapers and the headlines of the police journals.

Research has shown that it is crimes of violence that people most easily remember. Because they are spectacular, dramatic and terrifying, they obviously capture the attention and become more deeply rooted in the memory. Among the people questioned by Skogan and Maxfield (1981), who remembered a crime they had heard about several weeks before the inquiry, the cases many of them remembered involved brutal confrontations between the criminal and the victim. In 50% of the cases, it was a murder or attempted murder; in 5% it was a kidnapping or highjacking of an aeroplane and in 13%, a rape or other type of sexual assault. The other large category of criminal cases they remembered involved violence; they comprised assault or armed robbery (8%) as well as sexual abuse of children. Only 5% of the crimes recalled by the persons questioned concerned petty theft and robbery, yet these are not only the most common crimes and the most frequently recorded by the police, these are the crimes that claim the greatest number of victims.

These facts support what was previously said concerning the image people have of crime and criminals. There is another element, however, that has not been mentioned, and that is the effect of the indirect means by which people are informed of criminal and judicial facts. As Skogan and Maxfield (1981) note in their study, the information — whether it comes from other persons or the "media" — constitutes "indirect victimization" in that it directly affects the public's fear of crime. It is only logical that if the "media" transmits only facts about crimes of violence, people will only remember crimes of violence. The result, as we have seen, is a distorted view of criminals and the crime situation that can increase public fears — particularly those of the elderly who rely more than others on the mass media.

WORLD VIEW AND PERCEPTION OF JUSTICE

Perception of the crime situation, the fear of crime, the dread of victimization and images of the criminal justice system should all be placed in the perspective of the world view held by the elderly person. If not, the analysis loses part of its validity and explanatory value.

The G.R.A.C. study (1984) shows that, generally speaking, the senior citizens who made up the Canadian sample were more pessimistic than the rest of the population. In fact, among the respondents who were 60 and over, 24% thought that their personal life, at the time of the survey, was worse than it was five years previously (against 10% among the 30 and under). Similarly, there were 63% of senior citizens who considered that the conditions of life in Canada had deteriorated in the space of five years, whereas only 39% of the youngest age group (30 and under) shared this opinion. More old people than young (respectively 54% and 44%) felt that crime had greatly increased throughout Canada, in their city or in their neighbourhood. Older age groups were also more fatalistic; half as many (16%) as younger groups (33%) believed that something could be done to fight crime. With this attitude, they had little interest in the fight against crime — perhaps a little less than the rest of the population. There were only 7% of senior citizens who participated in prevention programs compared with 16% among the 30 and under group.

This pessimism and fatalism that seems to be associated with the current older age cohort may be largely due to a view of the world characterized by resistance to changing values and the erosion of traditional institutions. Some senior citizens may develop a feeling of alienation from society. Some of them are wary of change, would rather leave it to the experts to solve social problems, and feel that today's many conflicting values are beyond their understanding and their ability to change anything. Our data show a statistically significant difference between this attitude of senior citizens and that of younger members of the population: the older people think (1) that it is better to keep things as they are rather than try anything one cannot be sure of; (2) that people would be better off leaving society's problems to the experts; (3) that there are so many life-styles today there is no longer any way of knowing what to do; (4) that people are what they are, and there is no way they can be changed.

These four points of view are strongly enough interrelated (alpha = .66) to form an alienation scale indicating a lost grasp of reality and refuge in the past. Furthermore, this "alienation" scale is closely associated with greater conservatism and a more punitive approach. Our data show that the older the respondents, the more they resist change, the less tolerant they are[1] and the more they are in favour of punitive measures[2].

Given their conservatism and their feeling of alienation, senior citizens have a greater tendency to trust institutions and turn to them in need. The older people are, the more they show satisfaction with the police, for instance[3]. They are also more inclined to deny that the justice system is discriminatory or unequal. Consequently, fewer in number (24%) than younger people (42%) think the justice system favours the rich over the poor. Their respect for the institutions and traditional values leads them to have a positive attitude toward the correctional agencies, on the one hand, and to adopt a more negative attitude toward any infringement of the law — hence toward delinquents and criminals. If the elderly on the whole are in favour of more severe sentences, it is because their conservative view of the world fosters greater punitiveness, and older people are generally more conservative than younger ones. But, there may be other contributing factors. Punitive attitudes quite possibly depend on people's views regarding punishment and its function. Many senior citizens, or 76% for example, consider the prisons "veritable hotels" compared with 45% for the 30 and under group. Does the fact of seeing imprisonment as a less harsh, cruel or severe punishment imply greater punitiveness?

We do not believe so. It seems more correct to think that punitiveness is a basic reaction that becomes a part of people's personality, fashions their beliefs and values, their view of the world and their ideology. As such, it would be an element that would play an active and important role in forming their image of crime and the criminal, on the one hand, and their perception of the penal system and the way it reacts to crime and the criminal, on the other.

CONCLUSION

Elderly persons base their idea of crime in Canada mainly on information conveyed by the media and on public discussion. It is not surprising, then, that their image of crime is one of violence (against the person) of which the amount according to them, is increasing dramatically. On the other hand, their view of crime at the local level, for instance, in their neighbourhood, is less abstract; it is based on concrete situations (activities of the police, suspicious persons, etc.) or very possibly on a direct experience of victimization. Here the image of crime is mainly one of crimes against property, which are the most frequent and appear to be much more likely to occur than personal assault.

These findings have important implications for crime policies. They show that social reactions of intolerance and punitiveness are principally determined by crimes of violence and much less by other criminal acts; furthermore, these reactions are greatly influenced by the image conveyed by the media. Therefore, when we speak of the punitive attitudes and intolerance of elderly people, it is important to remember that they are reactions to a relatively limited category of criminal acts (personal attack). Although this type of crime involves the elderly less frequently, it is the focus of their attention and, as a result, fear of crime becomes synonymous with fear of victimization.

NOTES

1. Gamma = .48; p = .0000
2. Gamma = .23; p = .0000
3. Gamma = .15; p = .001.

CHAPTER 4

VICTIMIZATION OF THE AGED

As we have said before, based on recent studies, it is now acknowledged that the elderly have a lower rate of victimization than younger members of the population (Solicitor General of Canada 1983, 1984, 1985; Hochstedler 1981). It is the young, in fact, from 12 to 19 years of age who are most often the targets of violent crime (LEAA 1974, *in* Smith 1979). The fact that there are fewer crimes against old people is borne out by the official statistics on crime as well as by victimization studies on the "dark number" — a term for the unknown crimes (Ward 1979). The Canadian Urban Victimization Survey (Solicitor General 1985c), despite prevailing perceptions of the frequency of victimization of elderly people, had shown that they were relatively rarely victimized: "The rates of violent and personal victimization of elderly people were about one-sixth those for all adult residents of the seven cities surveyed. Those in the 16 to 24 age group, the highest risk group, were twelve times as likely as elderly people to have been personally victimized" (p. 1). It is also acknowledged more and more that although people of 60 and over are less often the victims of attack, when they are, they suffer much more serious consequences than other age groups.

SOME GENERAL FACTS ABOUT TYPES OF VICTIMIZATION

Although the rate of victimization on the whole is lower for the aged, it varies with different types of crime. According to the results of the Canadian Urban Victimization Survey (Solicitor General of Canada 1983, 1984, 1985), of all the crimes committed against old people (60 and over), the greatest number were household thefts (26%), followed by break and enter (23%). Next came vandalism (17%), personal thefts (17%), assaults (10%), robberies (4%), motor vehicle thefts (3%) and finally sexual assaults, which represented only one half a percentage point. A study in Kansas City (Cunningham 1976; Smith 1979) found that the victims were often alone and poor. For example, 58% of the victims of theft with violence had incomes of less than $5,000 and 26% of the sample had been victims of this same type of crime more than once (Pope and Feyerherm 1976; Cook *et al.* 1978). These figures are extremely important, for they illustrate the basic pattern of the type of victimization experienced by older people. That is, the elderly stand a greater chance of being victims of crimes against property (theft, robbery) than violent crimes against their person, such as assault and battery, rape or homicide.

Other studies show that the most frequent crimes against the aged are petty theft, purse-snatching and wallet-stealing (Conklin 1976), and in the same proportion as other age groups (Cook and Cook 1976; Hindelang 1976). These conclusions are similar to those reported by Antunes *et al.* (1977), who state that there is little probability that elderly persons will be the victims of every form of crime. They are less exposed to violent crimes, for example, but more exposed to predatory crimes. As for the use of violence during the commission of petty offences, it is less likely than for other age groups; but if violence is used, it usually occurs in the home or nearby. Hochstedler (1981) shows similar results. He finds that compared with the rest of the population, the elderly have a lower rate of assaults and thefts with violence and the highest rate of thefts of purses or wallets. In a Canadian study sample (G.R.A.C. 1984), the highest percentage of crimes is concentrated on theft and is comparable to that of the rest of the population, whereas crimes of violence account for only 17% of the offences suffered by old people.

Concerning fraud, there are few data on the extent of the problem, but Smith (1979) estimates the annual losses of American citizens of 60 and over at four billion dollars. In California, 90% of the victims of fraud and breach of trust are persons 65 and over, the majority of them being women. The sale of non-existent land, the sale of miracle drugs and medicines, fraudulent investments, etc. are some examples of consumer fraud, and these are but a few of the types of fraud to which the aged fall victim.

CANADIAN STATISTICS ON VICTIMIZATION

The Canadian Urban Victimization Survey, carried out in seven Canadian cities by the Department of the Solicitor General in 1982, is the most complete study we have on the amount of crime in the urban milieu. The seven cities chosen for the survey were Vancouver, Edmonton, Winnipeg, Toronto, Montreal, Halifax-Dartmouth and St. John's. This survey furnishes the most comprehensive data for 1981 regarding crimes reported and not reported to the police by the victims, the risks of criminal victimization, the impact of crime, the attitudes of the public toward crime and criminal justice, as well as how the victims feel about their experience.

According to Bulletin No. 1 (The Solicitor General of Canada 1983), the sample comprised a total of 61,000 citizens questioned by telephone, and only on incidents that took place in 1981. For the population studied, this made it possible to compile an inventory of 702,200 attacks against persons 16 years of age and over and 898,400 attacks on property. Less than 42% of these offences were reported to the police. Furthermore, according to Bulletin No. 6 on "The Criminal Victimization of Elderly Canadians" (Solicitor

General 1985c), people of 65 and over were the victims of less than 2% of all crimes against the person, whereas the youngest age group (16 to 24) were the victims of almost half of these offences.

For purposes of the survey, criminal victimization was separated into two general categories, personal victimizations (assault and battery, sexual assault, robbery, personal theft) and household victimizations (break and enter, vandalism, motor vehicle theft or theft of household property). For each of the seven cities, the number of known crimes was compiled and the rate of crime per 1,000 inhabitants or per 1,000 households was calculated. In 1981, the Canadian population over 16 years of age in the seven cities was 4,975,900 (2,357,000 men and 2,618,900 women). The total number of crimes of a personal nature was estimated at 702,200, of which 352,300 were acts of violence. The total number of crimes against private property amounted to an estimated 2,424,900 (document #1984-40, Solicitor General). It is based on these data that the crime rates were calculated for the various infractions, according to each city, by age and sex. The data of the survey on urban victimization was compared with those of the study on public attitudes toward crime policies (G.R.A.C. 1984).

TABLE 4.1

CANADIAN RATES OF CRIME BY TYPE OF CRIME AND AGE GROUP (1981)

		Rate per 1,000 inhabitants (1) or per 1,000 households (2)			
Types of crime		30 years and under	31 years to 59	60 years and over	All age groups
Household thefts	(2)	239	169	48	172
Robbery	(2)	119	96	43	94
Vandalism	(2)	121	85	32	88
Personal theft	(1)	117	50	18	70
Assault	(1)	107	33	10	57
Motor vehicle theft	(2)	25	15	5	17
Armed robbery	(1)	18	5	5	10
Sexual offence	(1)	7	2	0.5	4

NOTE: Data were collected in seven Canadian cities: Vancouver, Edmonton, Winnipeg, Toronto, Montreal, Halifax-Dartmouth, St. John's. Canadian Urban Victimization Survey, Solicitor General of Canada. The data used in this Table were furnished in November 1984 by the Department of the Solicitor General of Canada. I alone am responsible for the interpretation of these data.

The analysis of the Canadian rates of crime, by type of crime and age group, clearly shows that the victimization rate for young people (30 and under) compared with that for older people (60 and over) are three to five times higher in the case of armed robbery, robbery and motor vehicle theft.

The differences are even greater for other types of crime. The rates of victimization are actually seven times higher among young people than among the elderly in the case of personal theft, four times higher for assault and 14 times higher for sexual offences. The Canadian Urban Victimization Survey's data shows conclusively that elderly persons who live in private households are much less likely to be victims of crime than are those who are 59 and under.

Looking at Table 4.1 we see that for all crimes, the rate diminishes with the age of the victims. By adding the rates per age group, we see that the average decreases considerably as the population concerned becomes older. Comparatively speaking, for persons from 31 to 60 we get an average rate that is 52% of that for the 30 and under group. For people of 60 and over, the average crime rate is no more than 20% of that for the youngest group. Table 4.1 also shows that for all age groups the crimes follow this same order. For example, for both the youngest and oldest groups, the household theft comes first in terms of frequency. On the other hand, for all age categories, sexual aggression is the least frequent crime.

Concerning abuse and assault, we see that the rate for elderly people, in the seven urban centres studied, was 10 per 1,000 population for persons 60 and over as compared to 33 per 1,000 population for those 31 to 60, and 107 per 1,000 population for those 30 and under[1]. Overall, victims are assaulted by strangers in 66% of the cases, by acquaintances in 29% and by relatives in 6% of the cases surveyed. Now, if we take elderly victims of 65 and over, as do the researchers of the Solicitor General (Solicitor General 1984-44), the proportion of assaults committed by strangers rises to 74%. In other words, only about two of every 1,000 persons in the elderly population surveyed had been victims of any assault or abuse by a non-stranger over the period of study (1981). For the other people (64 and under), the rate was approximately 20 incidents per 1,000 population. We must point out, however, that the telephone surveys are probably not the most effective way of gathering information of this type; individuals who are dependent and vulnerable to abuse may be unable to divulge such incidents to interviewers, and those living in institutions are not included in the sample.

VICTIMIZATION ACCORDING TO SEX AND MILIEU

Based on the research undertaken by G.R.A.C. on Canadian populations, 30% of the people (254 out of 817) had been the victims of a crime during the year preceding the survey. Among those 30 and under, 50% had been the object of an offence, among persons between 31 and 59 the percentage dropped to 39%, and for those 60 and over, the rate was 11%. This agrees with one of the findings of the Canadian Urban Victimization Survey (Solicitor General of Canada 1983, 1984, 1985), namely, that risk of victimization is inversely related to age. The differences between this distribution and that of the Canadian Urban Victimization Survey (cited above for the same age groups: 56%; 39% and 5%), are due to the fact that the samples for the two studies were different and the studies of victimization were not made at the same time. The sample for the government research included seven cities, whereas that of G.R.A.C. comprised three cities and three rural areas. Furthermore, the first research analyzed the amount of victimization in a year whereas the second, because of a much smaller population, took into consideration the offences that had occurred during the two years preceding the survey. In spite of these differences, there is a great similarity between the distributions of the incidents of victimization according to age group. G.R.A.C.'s research on public attitudes to crime enabled us to compare the victimization rates in the urban milieu and rural regions according to age group, as well as the rate by sex. To do this, we analyzed the acts of victimization that the persons concerned had suffered during the *two* years preceding the survey.

TABLE 4.2

VICTIMIZATION BY AGE, SEX AND MILIEU

	Number and percentage of acts of victimization									
	Women		Men		Urban		Rural		Total	
Age group	N	%	N	%	N	%	N	%	N	%
30 and under	76	20	113	30	175	46	14	4	189	50
31 to 59	58	16	88	23	111	29	35	9	146	39
60 and over	26	7	15	4	30	8	11	8	41	11
Totals	160	43	216	57	316	84	60	16	376	100

NOTE: A 1981 survey in the cities of Winnipeg, Toronto and Montreal and in the rural areas of Manitoba, Ontario and Quebec (G.R.A.C., N = 817). The data reflect those victimized among the sample during the two years preceding the survey (G.R.A.C. 1984).

Over a period of two years, the 817 persons questioned had experienced a total of 376 criminal acts. More men were victims than women (57% and 43% respectively). This difference is more pronounced among the 30 and under group where 30% of the young men were victimized as against 20% of the young women. The difference lessens with age (23% and 16% for men and women from 31 to 59) to become reversed among the oldest group (4% of the men and 7% of the women). Men evidently expose themselves more to the risk of victimization than women do, particularly when they are young. A lifestyle that includes frequenting bars and an ostentatious display of possessions are no doubt indications that they live more "dangerously". Men account for 60% of the crimes of violence, and of these, the large majority (56%) are in the 30 and under category.

Taking into account the type of victimization, the Canadian Urban Victimization Survey (1985c) found that, as in the case of other age groups, "elderly males were about three times more likely than elderly females to be robbed and assaulted. Elderly females, on the other hand, were much more likely than elderly males to be the victims of personal theft; there were 18 thefts per 1,000 elderly females as compared to 7 thefts per 1,000 elderly males" (p. 1).

We also found that the risk of becoming a victim is five times higher in urban areas than in rural areas. In fact, 84% of the crimes reported took place in urban areas (Winnipeg, Toronto, Montreal) whereas only 16% were committed in rural regions.[2] Curiously enough, in the villages, the age groups seem to be victimized in similar proportions. The percentages of crimes vary from 4% to 9%, whereas in the cities, the youngest groups are victimized close to six times more than the oldest group (46% to 8%). It would seem, then, that life in a rural area is quieter, that there is less opportunity for crime (fewer things to steal, not so many bars, etc.) and that there is stricter control of the community. Families know their neighbours and are more or less aware of everyone's comings and goings. The people lack the anonymity of the large city with its possibility of getting lost in the crowd and avoiding surveillance of any kind. The daily life and way of thinking could explain the big difference between the two environments.

THE CONSEQUENCES OF VICTIMIZATION ON LIVING CONDITIONS

The living conditions of the elderly tend to show how much more likely they are to suffer physically, financially and psychologically than other people when they are the victims of a crime. This hypothesis is questioned by some criminologists, among them Cook, Skogan, Cook and Antunes (1978). Their analysis of the data contained in the American national surveys of 1973 and 1974 leads them to conclude that old people, when victimized, do not suffer more severe physical consequences or greater financial losses than other age groups.

This conclusion, which is based on statistics, evidently does not take into account the psychological impact of victimization. On studying the mean value of the losses sustained during thefts, according to the age of the victim, they show that the elderly (1) have less chance of being the victim of a crime than other age groups; (2) that the losses they sustain, in round figures, are the same or less than those of other adults; and (3) that the relative value of these losses, in terms of monthly income, are the same or greater than for other categories of victims.

Again, based on statistics, assault and its consequences is analyzed for different age groups. This leads to the conclusion that, with regard to injuries, old people (1) are less often attacked than others; (2) have more chance of being injured if attacked; (3) have fewer injuries or broken bones; (4) suffer more from internal lesions, loss of consciousness, cuts and contusions; (5) do not require more general medical care than others; (6) do not pay more in medical fees; (7) do not need care involving great expense; even if (8) the cost of care represents a much greater proportion of their income than for other groups. For Cook *et al.*, if the elderly differ from others where victimization is concerned, it is not because they are old but because they are poor: "elderly victims are a special group more because of their lower incomes than because of some innate frailty" (p. 349).

Other researchers do not share the point of view put forward by Cook *et al.* (1978) and recognize an element of aging that makes victimization of the aged much more traumatic. According to Conklin (1976), even though most of the time elderly people do not try to resist their aggressors, the latter have a greater tendency to brutalize them than when the victim is younger. According to his data, however, it seems that force was used against old people more to push or knock them down than to punch them or beat them. Nonetheless, whereas 25.2% of the young victims had been injured and 19.7% had to be taken to hospital, the corresponding figures for older victims was 41.9% and 27.5%. Conklin concludes that the frequency and gravity of injuries increases with age.

Hahn (1976) states (1) that there is no such thing as petty crime against the aged; (2) that elderly victims should be treated with the same compassionate attention and be given the same mobilization of community resources as the victims of natural disasters. According to Hahn, the consequences of crime are almost always serious for this portion of the population, and he cites four different consequences that crime may have for the elderly: "(1) Physical damage and suffering. (2) Financial cost, and in many cases, disaster. (3) Emotional trauma, especially fear; and (4) Changes in life-styles, often involving further withdrawal, isolation and even death" (Hahn 1976, 123).

The Canadian Urban Victimization Survey (document #1984-51, the Solicitor General) shows that old people have relatively little probability of being injured during an attack. Less than 17% of elderly victims who suffered an act of violence were injured compared with 29% among young victims. However, of the victims in the national sample who had been injured, those who were 65 and over had required dental or medical treatment more often than the younger ones. Violence toward persons 65 and over, even though less frequent than toward others, has more serious physical consequences because the elderly are more fragile.

The relatively low rate of crimes against the aged should not lead us to minimize the problem. On the contrary, it must be judged at its true value, and to do this, it is essential to take into account the physical, mental and financial condition of elderly people. The Canadian Urban Victimization Survey (Solicitor General of Canada 1983, 1984, 1985) shows that when aged persons were victimized, there was a greater chance that they would suffer more serious consequences than other age groups. The ratio of more serious to less serious crimes was higher among the elderly than among younger people. The ratio of robberies to personal thefts, for example, was 30 to 100 among the elderly and only 15 to 100 among other age groups.

The loss of goods and the financial consequences of victimization are generally more severe for persons 65 and over. The average value of the goods stolen in the seven Canadian cities that were surveyed was greater for old people than for the population in general. Thus, even though the elderly are victims of crime less often than younger people, the consequences are more serious. In all cases of victimization that occurred in 1981, the losses suffered by those of 16 and 17 years of age represented 0.4% of their income, for those between 30 and 39 it was 0.7% and for the 65 and over group it was 1.4% (# 1984-38, Solicitor General of Canada). Actually, the average net loss in dollars was no greater for the elderly group than for the others, but because of their low yearly incomes, the losses calculated in percentages of their revenue were more than twice those of the other age groups.

Financial losses are much more distressing for older people than for any other age group because, as we have seen, their financial resources are more limited. Many live below the poverty level. According to data in the Canadian Urban Victimization Survey (Solicitor General of Canada 1983, 1984, 1985), the elderly form a specific group, not only because they are more fragile and more vulnerable, but because they are in the lowest income bracket. Hence, a theft means a much greater loss for them than for younger people who are well off. A theft of $120, for instance, from a young person who earns $12,000 a year and who lives with his or her parents does not mean the same as for an elderly woman who, on a similar income, has little opportunity to recoup her loss.

For older people who are without work and who rely on small fixed incomes, the material goods they have are not always replaceable. In many cases, therefore, theft means the loss of something that cannot be replaced, or only with difficulty, because it is too expensive (television, jewels, etc.) or is irreplaceable (family photographs, meaningful souvenirs, etc.). The theft of a purse and the loss of essential papers — medical insurance card, bus pass, identification, etc. — can create considerable inconvenience for elderly people and involve a great deal of trouble and energy to acquire new ones (Logan 1979). What might be a minor inconvenience for young people, can easily become traumatic for older people.

VICTIMIZATION AND INFORMING THE POLICE

To explain why elderly persons are less often the victims of crime than other age groups, some researchers (Corrigan 1981) cite the imprecision and sparsity of the official statistics, which do not report the age of the victims. Others believe that there appear to be fewer elderly victims because they do not report incidents that have happened to them to the police: many aging citizens are reluctant to report crimes against themselves for fear of reprisals. Their fear leads to reluctance to go to the police and makes them particularly vulnerable to revictimization (Friedman 1976). We know, in fact, that 25% of elderly persons in the United States have been victimized several times (Cunningham 1976). But Hochstedler (1981) states that, on the contrary, almost one half the senior citizens report crimes — a little in excess of the rest of the population.

In Canada, the Canadian Urban Victimization Survey (Solicitor General of Canada 1983, 1984, 1985) arrives at similar results. With the data given us by the Statistics Division of the Department of the Solicitor General of Canada, we have been able to establish the rate of crime-reporting by age and type of crime.

Looking at Table 4.3, we see that for all crimes and offences, the percentage of those that were reported to the police increases with the age of the complainant. In fact, 36% of the incidents reported were by victims of 30 and under, increasing to 47% for victims of 31 to 59, to reach 50% for the 60 and over group. There is a parallel between the increase in reports to the

TABLE 4.3

PERCENTAGE OF CRIMES AND OFFENCES REPORTED TO THE POLICE, FOR THREE AGE GROUPS (1981)

Type of crime category	Proportion of reported incidents by age			
	30 and under	31 to 59	60 and over	All age groups
All incidents of a personal nature	28	41	49	
All incidents with violence	31	46	55	
Sexual assault	37	39	*	38
Robbery	35	62	64	45
Assault	30	44	51	34
Personal theft	25	37	43	29
All incidents against domestic goods	46	50	51	
Break and enter	60	67	73	64
Motor vehicle theft	69	73	68	70
Household thefts	44	46	36	44
Vandalism	32	36	41	35
Overall % reported	36	47	50	42

NOTE: The data were compiled from statistical tables furnished by the Department of the Solicitor General of Canada. The figures total the answers of the samples in seven Canadian cities that were the subject of a survey on victimization (Vancouver, Edmonton, Winnipeg, Toronto, Montreal, Halifax-Dartmouth, St. John's). Survey made in 1982.

* The actual count was too low to make statistically reliable population estimates.

police and the increase in the age of the victims for almost all crimes, and in particular, for crimes against the person and acts of violence. The fluctuations according to age group are less significant for property offences. In the case of motor vehicle theft and household thefts, the percentage of reports to the police by senior citizens is slightly lower than for the rest of the population. In view of these findings, there can be no support for the view that the apparently less frequent victimization of the aged is due to the fact that elderly victims are less inclined to report incidents to the police. The Canadian Urban Victimization Survey, on the contrary, shows a greater propensity among 60 and over victims of crime to report them to the police.

VICTIMIZATION AND PUNITIVENESS

In studies on victimization, the theory if often expressed that there may be a connection between the fact of having been a victim and punitive attitudes (Figgie 1980; Stinchcombe *et al.* 1980; Baril 1983). At first it would seem quite natural that a person who had been robbed or assaulted would feel a greater need to take revenge than someone who had never been a victim of crime. It might be expected, therefore, that former victims would also have a more negative attitude toward criminals than non-victims.

This is not the case, however. It is the elderly, those who are the least victimized, who are the most punitive. Moreover, according to the results of the Canadian research done by G.R.A.C (1984), there is not one fact that establishes a statistically significant relationship between victimization and punitiveness. Not only is there no connection between the two, but it seems, rather paradoxically, that there is an unexpected negative relationship. Generally speaking, the fact of having been a victim results in a less punitive attitude. For example, our data show that there is not quite as high a percentage of victims (68%) as non-victims (77%) who say that "the sentences pronounced by the court are not severe enough". It almost seems as though the victimization "demystified" the criminal act ("it's less serious than we thought") and "destereotyped" the offender's image ("he's not a *gangster*, a hired killer, but a person like everyone else"). Victimological studies, notably that of Baril (1983), support this conclusion and confirm that, in general (apart from the most serious victimizations and the most traumatizing, such as rape or extreme violence) contact with crime lessens the fear of crime and makes the victims less severe toward offenders. It is as though the "unknown" upon becoming "known" appears less frightening, less threatening, hence creating less anxiety.

During a study on the aim of punishment, Warr and Stafford (1984) found a strong correlation between age and degree of "retribution". They put forward two reasons for this. The first is connected with the fact that there is also a strong negative association between education and retribution. The fact is that the youngest cohorts have a higher level of education.

However, the connection between age and retribution remains strong even if we take the level of education into account. A second explanation, advanced as a hypothesis, would be that feelings of retribution largely stem from anger, that is, anger at one's own victimization or, perhaps more important, that of significant others. Thus, the cumulative probability that a person (or someone close to him) had been victimized at some time evidently increases with age. This would explain a good part of the "age/retribution" relationship.

This, of course, is an explanation that is difficult to verify. Still another explanation is that punitiveness depends to a large extent on one's system of values, one's view of the world — in other words, on ideology. The survey by G.R.A.C. (1984) undertook to measure the degree of punitiveness among Canadians. This was accomplished by means of four questions concerning: the severity of sentences, terms of 25 years of imprisonment, prison life and the death penalty. For each of these four questions, the elderly were shown to be more punitive than other members of the population. Based on these findings, whose reliability is fairly high (alpha = 0.66), we created a scale of punitiveness. Using this scale, the sample was distributed according to age, sex and milieu, as shown in Table 4.4.

TABLE 4.4

THE IMPACT OF SEX, AGE AND ENVIRONMENT ON PUNITIVENESS (1981)

Percentages of subjects showing a high level of punitiveness among the following categories:				
Age group	Men %	Women %	Urban %	Rural %	Total %
30 and under	34	35	33	40	35
31 to 59	50	53	50	54	52
60 and over	54	53	52	60	54
Totals	47	47	45	52	47

Sample: N = 425 (52%), N = 392 (48%), N = 614 (75%), N = 203 (25%).

Pearson's Correlation between age and punitiveness for:
Sex: Women: $r = .19$; $p = .0000$ Men: $r = .21$; $p = .0000$
Milieu: Urban: $r = .21$; $p = .0000$ Rural: $r = .15$; $p = .0000$

NOTE: Survey carried out in 1981 in the cities of Winnipeg, Toronto and Montréal and in rural areas in Manitoba, Ontario and Quebec (G.R.A.C. N = 817).

It is clear from the above that there is no connection between punitiveness and sex since it is the same for both men and women. In both cases, however, the punitiveness varies and increases with age in identical proportions. The difference between the elderly, as a specific group, and others is that they have a more punitive attitude. Moreover, the correlations between age and sex are the most significant (see Table 4.4). It is not the fact of being a man or woman that distinguishes the people who are more punitive or less punitive, but whether a person is young or old. We find the same parallel in the case of the urban and rural regions.

In fact, the punitive attitudes of urban people and rural people are pretty much the same, even though there is a slight tendency for those in rural areas — for each of the age groups — to be a little more severe and slightly more punitive. The difference is small and fluctuates between 7% (for the 30 and under group), 4% (for the 31 to 59 year olds) and 8% (among persons of 60 and over). But for these urban and rural citizens, the most significant variation occurs across the age groups and according to a pattern similar to that observed in the correlations between punitiveness and sex. Moreover, the correlation between age and place of residence is also significant in the case of people who have a highly punitive attitude.

PUNITIVENESS AND VIEW OF THE WORLD

In terms of general attitudes, the information gathered from the 817 Canadian respondents (G.R.A.C. 1984) leads us to conclude that the groups or individuals who show the most punitiveness are those who are the least liberal. We note that the persons in our survey sample who would like the penal system to be more severe with criminals are, in large measure, those who have a more rigid, more conservative, less tolerant view of the world. For example, the more punitive people are:

(1) more in favour of an authoritarian government (68% against 48% of the less punitive) to better ensure public order;

(2) more (64% against 49%) likely to believe that women with children should stay at home to look after them;

(3) more likely to think (85% against 72% of the moderate or slightly punitive) that if things are bad today, it is because the family has ceased to play the same role it used to assume;

(4) more of the opinion (58% compared with 50% for the others) that today people have no respect for anything;

(5) more likely (47% against 26%) opposed to homosexuals being accepted in our society like everyone else.

It seems logical, then, to find that punitive and conservative people are — culturally — the most deeply rooted in the past, in ancestral values and institutions, and are most in favour of maintaining the established order and acquired rights. Most of the punitiveness of the elderly is not due to their greater fear of crime, but to their more conservative view of the world. We must therefore conclude that there is a strong relationship[3] between age and the "conservative/liberal" variable (defined by the five points just enumerated).

Table 4.5 shows the relationship between age and view of the world, using the variables of sex and place of residence. Thirty-seven percent of the respondents who were 30 and under were more "conservative" than liberal, of those 31 to 59, 63% were more conservative and among those 60 and over, 84%. This increase in conservatism with age is true of the women as well as the men and in the urban as well as the rural areas.

TABLE 4.5

RELATIONSHIP BETWEEN AGE AND LEVEL OF "LIBERALISM/CONSERVATISM" (1981)

| Age group | Proportion of respondents highly conservative | | | | |
	Women %	Men %	Urban %	Rural %	Total %
30 and under	28	44	35	44	37
31 to 59	64	63	61	68	63
60 and over	92	73	82	89	84
Totals	61	59	58	67	60

Sample: N = 425 (52%) N = 392 (48%) N = 614 (75%) N = 203 (25%) N = 217 (100%).

Pearson's Correlation between age and conservatism for:
Sex: Women: r = .51; p = .0000   Men: r = .28; p = .0000
Milieu: Urban: r = .41; p = .0000   Rural: r = .36; p = .0000

NOTE: Survey carried out in 1981 in the cities of Winnipeg, Toronto and Montréal and in rural areas in Manitoba, Ontario and Quebec (G.R.A.C. N = 817).

The elderly women are more traditionalistic (92%) than the men (73%) and the old people in rural areas a little more conservative (89%) than those in the cities (82%). We learn, too, from this survey that there is a strong positive correlation[4] between conservatism and punitiveness. Among the people who were highly punitive, 56% were more conservative and 34% more liberal (G.R.A.C. 1984). Age and punitiveness were found to be closely linked as well[5].

In looking again at the five points on the "conservative/liberal" scale, the reader can see that each one shows a relationship with age, view of the world and, as a consequence, punitiveness (a direct connection between severity and conservatism has already been seen). Generally speaking, then, we can say that the current cohort of older people is:

(1) more in favour of an authoritarian government to better ensure law and order (70% of those 60 and over against 48% of those 30 and under);

(2) more in favour of women with children staying home to look after them (84% of the elderly compared with only 29% of the youngest group);

(3) more likely to believe it is because the role of the family has changed that things are bad today (93% against 67%);

(4) more likely to have the impression that people have no respect for anything today (72% and 46% of the elderly and under thirties, respectively);

(5) more against homosexuals being accepted in our society like everyone else (48% against 21%).

Elderly people's attitudes demonstrate that they are more conservative when it comes to values such as law and order, authority, women staying home, family unity, respect, and objection to sexual deviance. Younger people, on the other hand, are more open to change; they are more in favour of a flexible and less authoritarian government and more tolerant of other ways of thinking and lifestyles. These differences in points of view that characterize the various generations clearly show why the elderly are more punitive than other age groups.

What these findings indicate is the undeniable fact that any research on the attitudes of the elderly toward crime and criminal justice cannot be complete without a thorough study of their living conditions and view of the world. The fear of instability engenders a strong resistance to change and greater confidence in "the experts" to solve social problems. Furthermore, greatly perplexed by the many different life-styles today and the co-existence and confrontation of diverse systems of value, some elderly people may alienate themselves from the modern world. This clearly emerges in the answers to a series of questions that were part of the Canadian survey carried out by G.R.A.C. (1984). Here, 62.8% of those 60 and over, or three times the number of respondents of the 30 and under group (20.3%), said it is "better to keep things as they are rather than try things we are not sure of". Similarly, twice as many old people (51%) as young ones (25%) felt it was better for citizens to leave "the problems of society to the experts", while the majority of them (71%), versus less than half the younger people (48%), were of the opinion that "there are so many lifestyles nowadays that is is impossible to know what is right".

Every society, every group or every individual tries to create an image of the world that will give it meaning. This image, or this view which has been built more or less on human experience, finds support in the reality but interprets it in various ways. This is why the same event, or same situation can be interpreted differently depending on each one's norms and values, one's beliefs and previous experiences. The dynamics of the attitudes and behaviour of the elderly toward crime, and solutions to the crime problem, cannot be understood and reconstructed without studying and analyzing the normative system of images that mediate and determine them.

CONCLUSION

Canadian studies clearly show that elderly persons are victims of crime far less than other age groups. When they are victims of aggression, it is not so much acts of violence but crimes against property to which they are subjected. This does not mean that the victimization of elderly citizens should be minimized. On the contrary. It is a very serious matter, for the consequences for people of 60 and over are a great deal more serious (financially, psychologically and physically) than for younger people.

What is very important is that victimization of the elderly, in their case, has a marked influence on the quality of life. The fear of crime engenders anxiety which, as discussed in the next chapter, colours the entire lifestyle of the elderly. In a way, for this age group, the fear of crime becomes more important than crime itself.

People of 60 and over are found to be more punitive than others, not because they are often victimized — they are least victimized of any social group — but because of a world view that is more "conservative", more firmly set in the past and more deeply rooted in "traditional values".

NOTES

1. The Statistics Division of the Department of the Solicitor General of Canada furnished us with its results compiled according to the age groups already established; thus we were able to determine the rates of victimization according to both age and category of crime.
2. These were Cameron, Wallace, Cypress and Rosser for the Province of Manitoba; the agglomerations of Townsend and Middleton for Ontario and the villages of Warwick, Ste-Clothilde and Potton for Quebec.
3. Gamma $= .48$; $p = .0000$
4. Gamma $= .34$; $p = .0000$
5. Gamma $= .23$; $p = .0000$

CHAPTER 5

THE FEAR OF CRIME AMONG THE ELDERLY

Public discourse, at the present time, seems to want to link three phenomena — the increase in violent crime, the growing fear of crime and public demands for more repressive control measures. Although there appears to be a direct connection between the three, criminological research in this field indicates that the situation is not as simple as it may seem. For example, studies in Canada (G.R.A.C. 1984) and the United States (Stinchcombe et al. 1980; Skogan 1977; Adams and Smith 1976) confirm that women and old people, although victims of violent crime less often than others, are more frightened. On the other hand, studies indicate that persons who have been victimized have no greater tendency than anyone else to want more repressive measures. However, as it has been shown, old people are more punitive than others, due to the fact that there is a very strong connection between a person's view of the world — "conservatism/liberalism" — and punitive attitudes. The latter relate less to age than to an ideology; more people in our cohort of elderly persons were found to be "conservative" than in the other age groups.

THE FLUCTUATIONS OF VIOLENCE

In the United States, between 1962 and 1980, the rate of violent crimes (murder, rape, theft with violence and assault and battery) more than quadrupled, from 140 to 581 per 100,000 inhabitants. In Canada, during the same period, there were three and a half times as many crimes of violence as in the earlier period (Bellot and Elie 1983). These figures are well publicized by the mass media, creating a veritable crime psychosis in some of the population. According to Stinchcombe et al. (1980) however, victimization studies estimate that less than 2% of the American population (over the age of 12) had been the victims of violence during the year 1973/74. It is interesting to note, moreover, that even though by the late 70s, the increase in crimes of violence in both countries was slowing down, people's feelings of insecurity seemed to be increasing more and more. In the United States the rate of violent crime rose on an average of 13% a year between 1962 and 1970; it fell to 6% a year from 1971 to 1975, and to 4% a year from 1976 to

49

1980. In Canada we see exactly the same trend. The average annual increase in violent crimes was 11% between 1962 and 1970; 9% between 1971 and 1975, and only 2% a year between 1976 and 1980. We must not forget either that crimes of violence represent only an infinitesimal part of all crime. In fact it only represents from 3% to 10% of all criminal acts, depending on the country. In Canada, in 1983, for every 100 Criminal Code offences reported by the police eight were violent crimes. This category of offence experienced a slight increase (2.2%) between 1982 and 1983 and increased by 16.8% over the last five-year period (1979–1983). In terms of rate per 100,000 population, there was no change between 1982 and 1983 (Statistics Canada 1985; Catalogue 85-205).

The increase in violence, although relative, is nevertheless real, especially in large cities where crime is highly concentrated. In France, according to Peyrefitte (1981), the thirty odd million citizens who live in cities with more than 100,000 inhabitants are the victims of seven times more serious crimes than the rest of the population. In Canada, in 1983, the rate of crimes of violence was between 800 and 850 for urban centres of more than 100,000 inhabitants, whereas for medium-sized cities, it was about 700. In smaller places, those of less than 10,000 inhabitants, and in rural areas, the rate of violent crimes fluctuated between 500 and 600 per 100,000 inhabitants (Statistics Canada: Canadian Crime Statistics 1985). Thus, the majority of crimes and particularly violent crimes, occur in the large cities. In the United States, in 1981, 80% of all murders, rapes and armed robberies were committed in cities of 50,000 and more inhabitants, and these cities represent less than half the population (41%). Twice as many crimes as anywhere else, then, were committed in these cities. However, property thefts are more evenly distributed in American society. For the same year, according to the figures furnished by Skogan (1983), about 58% of all burglaries occurred in large urban centres as opposed to the 80% for violent crimes.

Surveys on public attitudes to crime show that there is a parallel between the extent of crime and the fear of crime. Skogan reports that an American enquiry, carried out in 1982, showed that 32% of the inhabitants of rural areas and small towns said they were concerned or worried about crime. This proportion rose to 42% among the inhabitants of medium-sized cities and to 71% among those living in large cities. In Canada, the Group for Research on Attitudes toward Crime (G.R.A.C.) found a less acute situation. Twenty percent of the people in rural areas were anxious about crime compared to 44% of those living in cities. Of these urban dwellers, 57% were women and 17% men (G.R.A.C. 1984).

THE FEAR OF CRIME — OR WORSE!

Most of the time people's fear is entirely out of proportion to the actual risks involved. In the United States, according to the Figgie Report, 17% of the citizens fear being murdered, whereas only one in 10,000 persons ever suffers such a brutal end (0.009% of the population); 55% of women are afraid of being raped, a proportion 900 times higher than the percentage of those who are (0.06%); people who fear being the victim of theft with violence (23%) are 120 times more numerous than the actual victims of this type of crime (0.19%). Some people are afraid of being attacked by a stranger outside their home, but as Conklin notes (1981, 64), there is at least ten times less chance of a person dying at the hands of a stranger than being killed in an automobile accident. People seem to be unaware of the fact that many crimes of violence are committed by persons who know one another and, in some cases, are related.

In a study in Philadelphia on murders, Wolfgang (1958) has shown that only 12% of the cases involved persons who were strangers to one another. Even more, in 25% of the murders, the victim and murderer were members of the same family. Conklin (1981) mentions a study in Washington, D.C., which came to the conclusion that only a third of the victims of rape and only 19% of the victims of sexual assault had been attacked by strangers. Proportionately, the same is true of Canada.

According to Canadian statistics, about one third of all murders occur within families. Another third involve social or business associates. For the remaining third, either there is no relationship (20%) or the case has never been solved by the police (close to 13%). Thus, the probability of being killed by a person you know is much greater than that of being murdered by a stranger in the street. As discussed, a great number of crimes that elicit a good deal of fear are committed by persons the victim already knows, and most often trusts. Much the same pattern holds for abuse of the elderly, which will be discussed later.

With regard to people's perception of crime, we find that it is distorted by the belief that most crimes are accompanied by violence. A survey undertaken by the Toronto Centre of Criminology (Doob and Roberts 1983) among a large sample of the population (N = 2,000) shows that about 75% of Canadians over-estimate the proportion of violent crimes. Whereas the statistics indicate that only 8% of crimes are violent, 75% of Canadians think that more than half of all criminal acts are accompanied by violence, that is, six times more than is actually the case. The public's perception of crime, therefore, bears little relation to the actual Canadian crime situation.

In Canada, where almost the total population has access to American television, it seems that people's opinion of the crime situation reflects an American view more than a Canadian view. This is the conclusion arrived at by Doob and Roberts (1982), who state that the Canadian public's view of the extent of the crime problem suggests that most members of the public see serious crime as more of a problem than it appears to be. Canadians vastly over-estimate the proportion of violent crimes; they think that we are closer to the United States in this regard than in fact we are; they think the number of murders has increased over the past six years when, in fact, it has not, and they believe that people released from prison on parole are more likely to commit crimes of violence soon after release when, in fact, this is not the case. The "mass media", and particularly television, convey the violence and consequent fear that exists in the United States. This, at least partially, forms the image that people on the Canadian side of the border may have of crime in general.

This distorted view of crime is obvious where murder is concerned. Close to two thirds of the Canadian population mistakenly believe that murder rates have increased since the abolition of capital punishment. In 1975, however, the year preceding the abolition of the death penalty, 701 murders were committed, whereas in 1982, six years after the abolition of the death penalty, 670 cases of homicide were recorded. In absolute numbers, then, homicides had diminished in Canada, the rate per 100,000 inhabitants going from 3.09 to 2.72 over the same period. The repeal of the death penalty, then, did not have the harmful consequences expected by many. Although it seems to have had no effect on the commission of murder, nonetheless, the public continues to believe the opposite. Unfortunately, however, no effort has been made by the Justice Department or the mass media to correct this erroneous impression and to better inform the population — perhaps even to change public attitudes as well.

EXPOSURE TO RISK, VICTIMIZATION AND FEAR OF CRIME

At the present time, there are many points that are unexplained in the analyses by criminologists on the victimization of elderly people. This is because there is a lack of research essentially concerned with the problems of this age group. In the United States, most of the information is derived from studies of the results of the regular surveys undertaken by L.E.A.A.[1] Putting aside the differences of opinion among researchers, however, which most often occur because of the confrontation between quantitative and qualitative methodologies, there appears to be consensus regarding the following points:

(1) Older people are victims of crime less often than other adult age groups (Skogan 1980);

(2) Older people are more afraid of crime than other age groups (Adam and Smith 1976) and this fear seems to increase with age.

This apparent paradox can be explained by the argument that, since elderly people have a greater fear of crime than other people, they isolate themselves more, and are thus less exposed to crime; hence their lower rate of victimization.

Lindquist and Duke (1982) are of the opinion that to the extent that "exposure to risk" can be weighed, the elderly have a rate of victimization either equal to or much higher than other age groups. The fact that they feel there is a strong probability that sooner or later they will be victims of crime, even though they are less often attacked, shows that they have a true picture of reality (Lawton 1980); in other words, they are one of the most vulnerable age groups. This engenders a greater fear that forces them to restrict their activities (Hahn 1976). The fear of crime, more than the crime itself, is typical of older people. As Clemente and Kleiman note (1976, 207), "It is reasonable to argue that for older people fear of crime is even more of a problem than crime itself." This assumption has yet to be verified, as well as elaborated upon, especially by ascertaining exactly what it is the elderly fear.

According to American surveys, the fear of crime (measured by the fear of walking alone at night) was not only greater for the oldest age group, but the proportion of elderly people who were afraid increased with time more than citizens who were aged from 18 to 25. Between 1965 and 1974, the proportion of elderly persons who expressed fear was 38% in 1965, 33% in 1967, 41% in 1968, 46% in 1973 and 56% in 1974. Among the young people, during the same period, the percentages were 35%, 30%, 37%, 40% and 43% respectively. Cook (1980) felt that the most important factor about these figures was the ever-increasing gap between the young and the old. In 1965 and 1966 the difference in the percentages of those in each age group who said they were afraid was about 3%; in 1968 it rose to 4%; in 1973 it was 6% and in 1975 it jumped to 13%. Thus, the ever-increasing fear of crime among the elderly gets farther and farther away from that of young adults. It seems to be generally accepted that the fear of crime is greater among the elderly than among young people. However, Skogan (1980) thinks that this is due less to age than to sex. According to him, the disproportionate concentration of women among the 65 and over group is a factor that distorts the picture and exaggerates the positive relationship between fear and age.

All the Gallup polls and all the L.E.A.A.'s surveys have proven that, compared with men, a greater proportion of women are afraid to walk alone at night in their neighbourhood. Between 1967 and 1977, the percentage of apprehensive women increased from 46% to 63%. During this same period of time, the men fluctuated between 16% and 23%. On the whole, in the United States, there are always almost three times as many women as men who fear crime (Stinchcombe *et al.* 1980). The study by G.R.A.C. (1984) shows that 26% of the persons questioned (213 out of 817 Canadian respondents) can be considered apprehensive, since they said that "often" or "very often" they avoided going out alone at night because they were afraid of a criminal attack. Among these, 84% were women (N = 179) and 16% men (N = 34); and among the women, there were more elderly persons (29% of them were over 60) than among the men (6% were 60 and over).

According to a survey in Seattle, Washington, Warr (1984) concludes that most of the variation in fear among the age/sex groups is due to some differences in the relation between fear and perceived risk:

... differences in the relation between fear and perceived risk among these groups demonstrate what might be called *differential sensitivity to risk*. Confronted with equal (apparent) chances of victimization, females and older individuals will still display higher fear than their counterparts, and, indeed, they may do so even if their perceived risk is lower (pp. 694–695)

These data would seem to substantiate Skogan's theory that sex more than age explains the fear of crime among the elderly. However, if sex influences the distribution of the fear of crime among old people, it is not because the women outnumber the men in this age bracket (Skogan's argument) but rather that elderly women are disproportionately more fearful than elderly men.

THE FEAR OF WALKING ALONE IN THE NEIGHBOURHOOD AT NIGHT

In answer to the question "Here, (where you live) do you feel very safe, fairly safe or not safe at all?", 90% of the persons surveyed in the cities of Toronto, Montreal, Winnipeg and in rural areas of Ontario, Quebec and Manitoba, said they felt "very" or "fairly" safe in the area in which they lived. This immense majority is made up of young people as well as persons 60 and over. A person's feeling of security depends largely on one's surroundings, one's activities and living habits, and in a way, is an indication of the degree of adaptation to the immediate environment. This does not mean that everyone feels safe for the same reasons. Young people may feel perfectly safe in every part of their area whereas the elderly may feel safe only at home or close to home. In this regard, the Canadian Urban Victimization Survey (Solicitor General of Canada 1983, 1984, 1985) gives us some interesting information, which we have briefly outlined in Table 5.1.

TABLE 5.1

FEELINGS OF SAFETY WHEN WALKING ALONE IN ONE'S NEIGHBOURHOOD FOR THREE AGE GROUPS (1981)

Percentage of persons, by age group, who feel safe or unsafe when walking alone in their neighbourhood				
	During the Day		After Dark	
Age Group	Safe	Unsafe	Safe	Unsafe
30 and under	96%	4%	63%	37%
31 to 59	95%	5%	62%	38%
60 and over	92%	8%	46%	54%
Total Population:	95%	5%	60%	40%

NOTE: The data were compiled from statistical tables furnished by the Department of the Solicitor General of Canada. The figures total the answers of the samples in seven Canadian cities that were the subject of a survey on victimization (Vancouver, Edmonton, Winnipeg, Toronto, Montreal, Halifax-Dartmouth, St. John's). Survey made in 1982.

It is clear that, in light of these answers, there is no characteristic that dichotomizes the persons of 60 and over and the rest of the population regarding a feeling of safety in the neighbourhood during the day. The G.R.A.C. research (1984) obtained the same results. When it was a question of feeling safe in general in the neighbourhood, 90% of the elderly (like the other age groups) felt safe. The story is different with regard to going out and strolling in the area after dark. Then, in comparison with the others, the elderly have a much greater fear. During the day their fear is almost the same as the others (8% to 5% and 4%). After dark, everyone's fear increases, from 4% among the 30 and under group to 37%, and among the 31 to the 59 group, from 5% to 38% (8 and 9 times greater respectively). Among the oldest, fear increases in similar proportions, from 8% during the day to 9 times more (54%) after dark.

What do people actually fear? Although most studies do not define "fear" explicitly, what they most often mean in this context is the feeling a person has that he may become the victim of a crime. As Sundeen and Mathieu (1976b) suggest, the fear of crime is "the amount of anxiety and concern that persons have of being a victim" (p. 55). In studies of victimization, the classic question that has been asked in surveys since 1948 in order to measure the fear of crime is one whose results we have just studied, namely: "Is there any area right around here — that is, within a mile — where you would be afraid to walk alone at night"?

Table 5.2 shows that, in the 30 and under age group and the 31 to 59 group there is no significant change in the proportion of women (48% and 35%) and men (7% and 6%) who avoid going out at night for fear of crime. The fear of going out after dark for these two groups remains stable, whether they live in cities (26% for the 30 and under bracket and 24% for the 31 to 59 bracket) or in rural areas (11% and 15% respectively). It seems that it is persons of 60 and over whose fear increases most, but only for

TABLE 5.2

RELATION BETWEEN AGE AND AVOIDING GOING OUT ALONE AT NIGHT FOR FEAR OF CRIME (1981)

Percentage of subjects who often or very often avoid going out at night for fear of crime				
Age group	Women %	Men %	Urban %	Rural %	Total %
30 and under	48	7	26	11	22
31 to 59	35	6	24	15	22
60 and over	60	17	51	11	41
Totals	42	9	30	13	26
Sample	52	48	75	25	100

NOTE: Survey done in 1981 in the cities of Winnipeg, Toronto and Montreal and in rural areas of Manitoba, Ontario and Quebec (G.R.A.C. N = 817).

those living in the cities. For the 31 to 59 year olds who live in a city, 24%
are afraid to go out at night, and for the 60 and over group, 51% are afraid,
whereas the percentage is less in the country (it falls slightly from 15% to
11%). Although it increases for both sexes, and in similar proportions, the
proportion of fearful women is much higher than that of the men. In fact,
among the 60 and over group, the percentage of fearful women almost
doubles, going from 35% for the 31 to 59 age group to 60%. For the men of
this age group it jumps from 6% to 17%. This shows, as most surveys have
found, that a person's milieu and age strongly influence his or her fear of
crime.

CONCRETE FEAR AND FORMLESS FEAR

The Figgie Report (1980) in the United States examines two types of fear,
which it defines as a "concrete fear" of being the victim of acts of violence
and a "formless fear" of some vague threat to one's security. It establishes
an index for each of these types of fear.

Concrete Fear Index

This indicates the intensity of a person's fear *vis-à-vis* six major crimes; the
fear of being murdered, of being sexually assaulted or raped, of being
mugged, knifed, beaten up, and being held up by an armed robber.

Formless Fear Index

This acts as a barometer of the fear a person may have of indeterminate
threats he feels are lurking in his surroundings: fear of being alone during
the day or at night in the central business district or main shopping centre,
or of being alone during the day or night in the neighbourhood or at home.

An analysis of the distribution of these indices, according to age, in this
American study, shows that concrete fear is significantly connected with
age[2]. Concrete fear is higher among young people than among the elderly.
On the other hand, there is a relationship between formless fear and isolation. The elderly, part-time employees, widows and widowers, divorcees
and people who are separated, experience higher degrees of unspecified
fear. It seems that the less people are involved in the social activities of their
community, the more they suffer this type of nameless fear.

Young people are the most strongly affected by the concrete fear of being
victims of crime. Almost half say they fear being the object of a violent
attack. This fear diminishes with age, for 40% of the 31 to 59 group say
they are afraid against 33% of the older people. It seems, then, that the fear
of violent crimes reflects the probability of real victimization, because of a
person's lifestyle, socio-demographic characteristics and degree of exposure
to risk. According to the F.B.I. Uniform Crime Report, persons from 20 to

29 represent 33% of murder victims, whereas they represent only 17% of the American population. Also, 55% of the women are afraid of being raped. In 1978 there were 67,000 cases of rape in the United States (Figgie 1980). The authors of the Figgie Report conclude that the people who show a high degree of *concrete fear* are: those who live in large cities, who are young, who in large part are female, who most often belong to black minorities and who, more than others, are exposed to the information propagated about crime by the mass media.

Older people are the most prone to fall victim to *formless fear*. In this age category (60 and over), there are more apprehensive individuals (43%) than in other age groups (36% and 35% respectively). Although the socio-demographic factors exercise an influence here as well, especially the fact of living in a large city, being Black or being a woman, what specifically influences this vague fear are unfavourable social conditions (low income, little education) and personal isolation (widowhood, unemployment, solitude). In short, financial, social and individual insecurity engenders general feelings of insecurity *vis-à-vis* crime. Since many elderly people most often live under difficult conditions, and frequently suffer from isolation, one can understand why they are more vulnerable to this nameless, but to them, very real fear. The survey carried out in Canada (G.R.A.C. 1984) arrives at similar results. The data in Table 5.4 have a striking resemblance to those of the Figgie inquiry shown in Table 5.3.

On comparing the two studies shown in Tables 5.3 and 5.4, we note that a strong concrete fear of being a victim of crime is no more frequent in the United States (41%) than in Canada (37%). For a high degree of formless fear, which affects 37% of Americans and 38% of Canadians, the same pattern holds for the two countries. Where differences appear, they are due to the distribution according to age. In the case of concrete fear, a high level affects 11% more of the 30 and under group in the United States (49%) than in Canada (38%). For older age groups, the two become closer and closer; a high level of concrete fear is found, respectively, among 40% of persons from 31 to 59 in the U.S., and 37% in Canada; for the 60 and over group, the two levels are exactly the same — 33%. In the two countries, then, concrete fear diminishes with age. It is the young who are more affected, precisely because their life-style exposes them to a much greater risk of victimization.

In the case of formless fear, the Canadian findings diverge a little from the American. The latter show that a vague fear, stable up to the age of 59, jumps from 35% to 43% among persons 60 years of age and over. In Canada, this type of fear is very high among 40% of young people, 33% of the 31 to 59 year olds and 46% among those in the 60 and over bracket. It not only affects more old people than in the United States, but also more young people. There are no cross-tabulated data in the Figgie Report (1980) by which we could compare the types of fear by age and sex. What this American study tells us is that a greater percentage of women show a high

TABLE 5.3

IMPACT OF AGE ON CONCRETE AND FORMLESS FEAR ACCORDING TO THE DATA OF THE FIGGIE REPORT (1980)

Age group	Concrete Fear				Formless Fear			
	High		Mod/Low		High		Mod/Low	
30 and under	139	49%	144	51%	102	36%	181	64%
31 to 59	205	40%	304	60%	176	35%	332	65%
60 and over	78	33%	158	67%	102	43%	135	57%
Totals	422	41%	606	59%	380	37%	648	63%
N = 1028								

NOTE: The data were compiled from statistics presented in the Figgie Report (1980).

TABLE 5.4

THE IMPACT OF AGE ON CONCRETE AND FORMLESS FEAR OF CRIME ACCORDING TO THE CANADIAN DATA (1981)

Age group	Concrete Fear				Formless Fear			
	High		Mod/Low		High		Mod/Low	
30 and under	90	38%	147	62%	94	40%	143	60%
31 to 59	149	37%	249	63%	131	33%	267	78%
60 and over	60	33%	122	67%	84	46%	98	54%
Totals	299	37%	518	63%	309	38%	508	62%

NOTE: Survey done in 1981 in the cities of Winnipeg, Toronto and Montreal as well as among rural populations in Manitoba, Ontario and Quebec (G.R.A.C. N = 817).

degree of concrete fear (46%) as well as vague fear (48%) than men (respectively 34% and 26%). Table 5.5 shows that in Canada, too, the percentage of fearful women is higher than that of men, and this is true of concrete fear (45% of women against 30% of men) as well as vague fear (57% of women against 17% of men). The table clearly shows, and particularly regarding formless fear, the predominance of women and especially elderly women.

An analysis of the Table 5.5 shows the differential impact of age and sex on the fear of crime. For the Canadian sample, the concrete fear of victimization is high among 45% of women and 30% of men. The difference is even greater where formless fear is concerned; it is high among 57% of the women compared to 17% of the men. In terms of the "fear/age" relationship, according to sex, Table 5.4 shows that concrete fear gradually lessens with age; it affects 38% of persons 30 and under, 37% of the 31 to 59 group and 33% of those in the 60 and over bracket. When these same results are examined taking sex into account (Table 5.5), a difference can be seen.

TABLE 5.5

IMPACT OF AGE AND SEX ON CONCRETE AND FORMLESS FEAR OF CRIME ACCORDING TO CANADIAN DATA (1981)

Age group	Concrete Fear				Formless Fear			
	Men		Women		Men		Women	
30 and under	49	33%	49	44%	28	22%	66	59%
31 to 59	46	25%	103	49%	26	14%	105	50%
60 and over	21	27%	39	38%	14	18%	70	68%
Totals	116	30%	190	45%	68	17%	241	57%

NOTE: Survey done in 1981 in the cities of Winnipeg, Toronto and Montreal as well as in rural areas in Manitoba, Ontario and Quebec (G.R.A.C. N = 817).

Among the men a high degree of concrete fear affects a third of the youngest group (30 and under) and a quarter of the older groups (25% of persons 31 to 59 and 27% of the 60 and over). Among the women it increases from 44% for the 30 and under group to 49% for those between 31 and 59. For those over 60 it falls substantially, dropping from 49% to 38%. It is obviously the fear of rape that accounts for this profile of the fear of victimization among women and for the differences that distinguish it from that of the men.

The formless fear of crime takes an altogether different course. It is high among 40% of young people of 30 and under, among 33% of persons aged 31 to 59, and among 46% of persons 60 and over (Table 5.4). It is highest among elderly women (68% of those 60 and over and a little more than half of the other age groups) (59% and 50% for the 30 and under and 31 to 59 respectively) (Table 5.5). Among the men, the feeling of insecurity remains constant and generally low: 22% of the youngest, 14% of the middle-aged group and 18% for the oldest.

These results seem logical and are in keeping with the living habits of the various age groups. Young people, more mobile and adventurous, go out more than old people — day and night — and often go to places where there is a much greater risk of victimization (discotheques, bars, the downtown area, questionable districts, the drug scene, etc.). This explains why they have a greater concrete fear of crime. Furthermore, in the 30 and under age group there are many more young girls (29%) than young men (21%) who think "often" or "very often" that someone could enter their homes and attack them. There is no doubt, moreover, that behind this fear is the fear of being raped.

The study by Warr (1984), in Seattle, tends to support this conclusion:

Still, it is reasonable to speculate at this point that rape may be the "master offense" in fear of victimization among women, and, indeed, it may well be that, for younger women in particular, fear of crime *is* fear of rape (p. 700).

FEAR OF CRIME AND SOCIAL INTEGRATION

A good proportion of senior citizens live alone. In the seven Canadian cities chosen for the Canadian Urban Victimization Survey (Solicitor General of Canada 1983, 1984, 1985), 40% of the men and 67% of the women 65 and over were living alone. In Montreal, for the same age group, 33% were living alone, 70% of them women (Brillon 1986). To this solitude is added some degree of social isolation. The studies of Sundeen and Mathieu (1976a, 1976b) suggest that there is actually an inverse relationship between social contact and fear of crime. The fewer the social contacts, the greater the fear. What matters most is not so much the fact of living alone as it is the isolation from all human contact.

Fear of specific crimes, such as burglary and theft with violence, is also linked with socal integration (Sundeen 1977). The dread of being burglarized is marked by a low level of community participation and a pessimistic estimation of the probability of help from neighbours in case of need. This negative assessment of the collaboration of neighbours is also associated with a special fear of burglary and fraud, in this case with a negative evaluation of the neighbourhood (it is not a good place in which to live). Pfuhl (1980) reports much the same thing. He finds a direct relationship between seeing the community as unstable and fear of crime and an inverse relationship between the degree of social support on the part of the community and fear. These two factors apply more to women; the men seem to be more affected by the number of friends they have: the fewer the friends, the greater their fear.

CONSEQUENCES OF THE FEAR OF CRIME

We assume that fear affects the behaviour of the elderly by preventing them from going out and by limiting their daily activities. This reaction could be seen more as withdrawal or avoidance than as the more active response of taking appropriate protection measures (Furstenberg 1972). There is always a doubt, however, about the sequence involved here. We do not know whether senior citizens go out less because they are afraid or whether they are afraid because they go out less. What is more certain is that fear of crime hardly seems to prompt them to take any prevention or protection measures.

The Canadian survey, done in the provinces of Manitoba, Ontario and Quebec (Brillon *et al.* 1984), indicates that very few people of 60 and over use concrete methods to prevent crime and protect their property. Only 10% have a guard dog against 20% for the rest of the population; only 22% have a chain on the door or a safety lock against 56% for other age groups, and only 14% against 22% for the under 30 group had recourse to operation identification in order to protect their valuables. This is in line with the conclusions of the Canadian Urban Victimization Survey (1985, Bulletin

No. 6), according to which the elderly are less informed than young people about community prevention programs (Neighbourhood Watch, Operation Identification, Block Parents) and consequently are less apt to participate in them.

AGING AND FEAR

Until very recently, when they dealt with the subject of fear, victimization surveys have often shown a lack of imagination. As discussed, since the 50s, the Gallup polls have used the same question to measure the fear of crime: "Is there any area right around here — that is, within a mile — where you would be afraid to walk alone at night?" As Stinchcombe *et al.* (1980) noted, this question applies only to the problem of street crime. It does not make a distinction between "perception of risk and the fear which that perception evokes" (p. 45). Moreover, on the basis of this question, there is no way of ascertaining the fear evoked by various types of crime.

We do not yet know whether this feeling of insecurity, this vague fear that is so prevalent among senior citizens, stems from their perception of the crime situation or is due to the aging process, or both. In this regard, we have hardly any data other than those we obtained from our Montreal survey (Brillon 1986). One of the questions we have tried to answer is whether or not there is a correlation between the fear of crime and the other sources of anxiety that might emerge with age. To answer this question, we constructed a scale of "general fear" composed of four concrete examples, namely fear (a) of having an accident; (b) of having no money; (c) of

TABLE 5.6

CONNECTION BETWEEN FEAR IN GENERAL AND DEPRESSIVE TENDENCIES (1983)

Depressive tendency	Degree of general fear				
	Very little fear N %	Some fear N %	Considerable fear N %	Great fear N %	Total N %
Slight	29 45	20 31	5 8	10 16	64 33
Fairly high	22 25	23 26	24 28	18 21	87 45
Very high	4 9	8 19	10 23	21 49	43 22
Totals	55 28	51 26	39 20	49 25	194 100

Gamma = .45; p = .0000 Sample: N = 210 (No answer: 16)

NOTE: Survey carried out on a Montreal sample of 210 persons of 60 and over. "General fear" measures the fear of accident, illness, solitude, poverty, and "depressive tendencies" measure low morale, disappointment and pointlessness of life (Brillon 1986).

becoming ill and (d) of being alone and isolated. The analysis shows that these four types of fear are interrelated since their coefficient of reliability Alpha is 0.63.

We find first, surprisingly enough, that this "general fear" among persons of 60 and over has no connection with either sex, income, solitude or even experience of having held a job. One might have thought that people who have previously worked, men or women, would perhaps have had more contact with reality and hence fewer anxieties. It would also seem logical that more affluent people and those who live with a mate or with their family (the majority of men) would be less likely to fear having an accident, a loss of money, illness or solitude. However, these are things that worry everybody, so they have little connection with living conditions.

On the other hand, "general fear" is quite closely connected with a person's psychological state. It is those who are most depressed about aging who have the highest rate of general fear. In our research, the fact of aging in a negative way is measured on a scale of depressive tendencies. This scale is composed of the following four descriptive states (coefficient of reliability Alpha = 0.63):

— Everything I do is pointless, boring
— The most difficult period of my life is right now
— When I look back, I find I've never done what I wanted to
— Compared to others, my morale is low.

Thus, in our Montreal survey sample of senior citizens, among those who are slightly "depressed", there are 16% who show a high degree of "general fear". Among those who have more marked "depressive tendencies", there are 49% who also have "great fear". The connection, then, is very consistent and significant[3]. The more disappointed, dissatisfied and defeated they are, the more these elderly people fear that misfortune will strike. It would have been interesting to see whether the same pattern is true for other age groups. It is to be hoped that future surveys on victimization will introduce a scale of "general fear" in order to study the connection between concrete fear and formless fear. This "general fear" in the elderly is also strongly correlated with an alienation scale[4]. This means that the senior citizens who show the greatest anxiety over change, who are the most confused by the many different existing values and the most inclined to leave social problems to the experts, are also those who have the highest level of "general fear".

What is interesting in this analysis is that "general fear" is also strongly associated with the scale of concrete fear as well as that of formless fear. During the Montreal survey, for each of these types of fear, scales were constructed similar to those Figgie used, which were composed as follows:

(a) *Scale of concrete fear*: For each respondent, it notes the degree of anxiety he feels *vis-à-vis* five delinquent acts, namely his fear of burglary, of being robbed in the street, of having his car stolen, that he will be attacked in his home and that he will be assaulted on the street. The degree of consistency of these five is high enough to construct a unidimensional scale (alpha = .73).

(b) *Scale of formless fear*: It measures the fear of undetermined threats that a person may experience in his daily life. For the Montreal survey, it is a question of the fear of going out alone at night; a feeling of insecurity in the neighbourhood; refraining from doing certain things for fear of crime; the desire to move to a safer neighbourhood; the degree of general concern about the crime situation (Reliability, alpha = .62).

Among people of 60 and over, there is a significant correlation between "general fear" and "formless fear"[5] on the one hand, and between "general fear" and "concrete fear"[6] on the other. There is also a strong correlation between "formless fear" and "concrete fear"[7]. This means, at least for the elderly, that all types of fear are interdependent. People who are most afraid of life in general have a greater tendency to feel insecure and to fear being a victim of criminal attack. However, the nature and extent of the links that connect all these various types of fear are yet to be explored and explained.

What the results of this Montreal survey indicate is that general fear, as we have seen, depends on the "morale" of elderly people, their degree of alienation, and to a lesser degree, their state of health. Formless fear, too, is due to depressive tendencies[8]; this is what seems to associate it with general fear. On the other hand, what makes it more specific, to all appearances, is the fact that it depends more directly on the living conditions. Formless fear is greater among women, persons living alone and those with low incomes[9].

With regard to concrete fear, it is because of its association with the level of alienation[10] that it seems to be linked with general fear. Compared with the other two types of fear, it appears to be much more active in influencing behaviour. Consequently, our data show that the fear of actual victimization is enough to encourage senior citizens to take more preventive measures[11]. These consist, among others, of having their home watched during a prolonged absence (a measure used by 56% of the respondents); having the lawn mowed or snow removed (18%); having the mail picked up or stopped (22%); leaving the radio on or lights lit to show that someone is home (65%); putting valuables in a safe place (38%); advising the police or superintendent of their absence (15%) and having someone occupy the home (11%). We also note that the greater the senior citizens' concrete fear, the more they tend to protect themselves[12]. These protective measures, in most cases, are limited to identifying objects of value (done by 12% of the sample), installing a safety lock (23%), putting bars on windows and doors (12%), increasing the outside lighting (8%), installing an alarm system (4%), and buying a dog (2%) or firearm (1%).

FEAR AND PUNITIVENESS

Most studies have shown that people's fear of crime does not seem to have any specific connection with a punitive attitude. People who are afraid of becoming victims have no particular tendency to demand more severe sentences for criminals. Proof of this is that, in the United States, women and Blacks — those most fearful of crime — are less punitive than men and Whites (Stinchcombe *et al.* 1980). The Figgie Report comes to the same conclusion:

> Our analysis reveals that support for specific punitive measures exists irrespective of levels of either concrete or formless fear. With regard to *both* types of fear, almost equal numbers of the fearful and non-fearful favor the death penalty and long prison sentences. The fearless are no more likely than the fearful to believe that long prison sentences discourage crime. (p. 127)

On the other hand, Figgie's research indicates that there are more elderly people (60 and over) in favour of the death penalty (76%) than others (71%) and particularly those under 30 (67%). The results also show that women (68%) are less in favour of capital punishment than men (76%). The Canadian study by the Group for Research on Attitudes to Crime (G.R.A.C. 1984), clearly shows that punitiveness varies with age[13]. Thus, we see that 54% of people 60 and over have a punitive attitude compared with only 35% of the 30 and under group.

One of the surprising results of the Montreal survey is the finding that there is actually a relationship between concrete fear and attitudes toward the death penalty.[14] This is no doubt because the survey's question on capital punishment was very specific, as Table 5.7 shows.

TABLE 5.7

RELATION BETWEEN CONCRETE FEAR AND ATTITUDES TO THE DEATH PENALTY (1983)

	Degree of concrete fear								
Opinion on the death penalty	Very little fear N	%	Some fear N	%	Considerable fear N	%	Great fear N	%	Total N	%
Totally against	16	53	4	13	3	10	7	23	30	14
Somewhat against	13	42	9	29	2	7	7	23	31	15
Somewhat in favour	24	39	6	10	13	21	18	30	61	29
Totally in favour	19	22	21	24	18	20	30	34	88	42
Totals	72	34	40	19	36	17	62	30	210	100

Gamma = .24; p = .0004
NOTE: Survey carried out on a Montreal sample of 210 persons of 60 and over (Brillon 1986).

The above clearly shows that among the entire population, there is a gradual increase in the percentage of respondents who favoured the death penalty. Hence, only 14% of this 60 and over group are totally against the death penalty, 15% are somewhat against, 29% are somewhat in favour of it and 42% are totally in favour of it. Of those who have a low score on the concrete fear scale, more than half are totally against the death penalty, whereas among the most fearful, there are only 23% against it. At the other end of the scale, among those who have very little fear of becoming victims of crime, only 22% are totally in favour of capital punishment compared with 34% of the very fearful.

These findings seem to show a direct relationship between fear of victimization (as we have defined it) and punitiveness among people 60 and over, at least if we go by their opinions on capital punishment. This is an area that should be studied more in depth. To date, the connection between fear, victimization and punitiveness has not been explored thoroughly enough. It should be analyzed, no doubt, in terms of the crimes (violent or non-violent) to which people have fallen victim, as well as the various levels of fear and different variables capable of defining punitiveness more precisely. These are basic elements that should be studied in order to understand better why older people are more punitive than other age groups.

CONCLUSION

We often tend to think that an increase in crime causes an increase in fear, and this in turn provokes a greater tendency toward more punitive attitudes. This is no longer true. For several years now the increase in crime has been found to be gradually slowing down (the rates seem to be stabilizing), whereas the public's fear of crime continues to soar.

Research done in Canada and the United States has shown that there is no direct connection between victimization and the fear of crime. For instance, in spite of the fact that elderly people are less often victims of crime than other age groups, they are much more fearful. This apparent paradox can be explained, at least in part, by the aging process, which leads many senior citizens to change their living habits. Since many of them go out less often at night, they are less exposed to the danger of becoming victims of aggression. That is why their rate of victimization is much lower than that of other age groups. Another factor, both physical and psychological, is vulnerability. Many aged persons are more fragile than younger people; hence they not only fear being incapable of defending themselves against a possible aggressor, but they also fear, above all, the serious consequences (financial, psychological and physical), should someone attack their person or rob them of their possessions.

As Warr (1984) clearly shows, what actually explains the high degree of fear among elderly citizens — fear we have qualified as formless in their case — is that in their eyes there are many offences that, while not serious in themselves, can cause extremely serious consequences. Warr refers to these offences as *"perceptually contemporaneous offences"*. This means that a single crime is perceived as a possible occasion for other crimes to be committed at the same time. Break and entry can be accompanied by vandalism, theft, assault and even homicide.

For example, for many women, the risk of burglary, even though the same for a man, can create far more fear because breaking and entering may be associated by some women with assault, rape and even homicide. The same act can produce a different intensity of fear in different people depending on whether or not it is perceived as being accompanied by more serious acts. Thus, elderly persons who meet a juvenile in the street may consider the possibility of danger, whereas adolescents would be far less likely to do so. If a person 65 and over feels that the slightest shove may have dramatic consequences, it is easy to see that many more crimes can be perceived by that person as opportunities for multiple offences.

Finally, let us keep in mind the studies analyzed in this chapter, which show that, among elderly citizens, the fear of crime is closely associated with insecurity which, in many cases, is part of the aging process. It is manifested, for example, in the fear of having an accident, of becoming ill, of being alone and not having enough money. Thus, the fear of crime seems to be closely linked with other fears that an aged person may have. The more the latter is afraid of life, the more he is afraid of crime. Another important finding is that there is a connection between mental health and various types of fear. The elderly subjects who have a greater tendency to depression are also those who are most afraid of crime. We also found that, among senior citizens, there is a relationship between concrete fear and attitudes in favour of the death penalty. These are results that should be of lively interest to researchers and all who work with the elderly because these are areas where attitudes are still not fully understood and should be studied further.

NOTES

1. Law Enforcement Assistance Administration (L.E.A.A.).
2. Gamma = 0.17
3. Gamma = .45; p = .0000
4. Gamma = .38; p = .0000. This alienation scale is based on the following four opinions: It is better to keep things as they are rather than try things we are not sure of; there are so many kinds of life styles today that we no longer know what to do; citizens had better leave the solving of society's problems to the experts; people are what they are, you can't expect to change them (coefficient of reliability Alpha = 0.72).

5. Pearson's correlation is $r = .25$ ($p = .0001$)
6. Pearson's correlation is $r = .32$ ($p = .001$)
7. Pearson's correlation is $r = .40$ ($p = .001$)
8. Pearson's correlation is $r = .18$ ($p = .005$)
9. Pearson's correlations between formless fear and these variables prove significant, since for sex, they are .30 ($p = .001$), for the degree of solitude, .24 ($p = .001$) and for income, .18 ($p = .006$).
10. Pearson's correlation is $r = .18$ ($p = .004$)
11. Pearson's correlation is $r = .18$ ($p = .005$)
12. Pearson's correlation is $r = .26$ ($p = .001$)
13. Gamma $= .17$; $p = .0004$
14. Pearson's correlation is $r = .23$ ($p = 001$)

CHAPTER 6

NEGLECT AND ABUSE OF THE ELDERLY

From a criminological point of view, the neglect and the abuse of old people are rather delicate matters. They are not always "crimes" in the legal sense of the term. The elderly may be victims of a series of abuses that are rarely exposed because they are subtly and secretly practised. The fact remains, however, that even though they may not constitute legal crimes, these negative attitudes and behaviour often do a great deal of harm, which seriously undermines the quality of life of elderly persons.

Abuse of the aged is not new, but it is only recently, with the increasing number of old people, that society has come to recognize the extent of the problem. If the problem is a matter of concern today when the elderly represent only 10% of the population, one can just imagine what it will be by the year 2025, when there will be nearly 5 million persons over 65, or about one fifth of the Canadian population. The present generation should be even more concerned since they will be the most directly affected.

The fact is that, whatever our age, at some time or other, we will be called upon either to support an aged parent, or — when we are old — be dependent on our children or the coming generation. As Steinmetz (1981) points out, even if it were possible to carefully plan one's financial resources, it would be unrealistic to think that most people would be able to spend their entire life without turning to their children or younger relatives for help. "Therefore", says the author, "it is critical to bring national attention to this problem in order to motivate researchers and social service professionals to gather data, exchange knowledge, and stimulate future research, education and policy-making that will provide for a comprehensive continuum of care for the elderly and their families" (p. 81). If nothing is done today to design policies and establish programs adapted to the demographic evolution, it will be much more difficult 10 or 20 years from now to furnish the aged with decent conditions of life.

During the 60s, public attention was drawn to child abuse and to counter it, the government adopted preventive measures and established assistance services. In the following decade the same thing occurred with regard to domestic violence and wife battering. Now, as King (1984) points out, it is the neglect and abuse of old people, most often by the younger members of their family, that have emerged as serious and widespread forms of family violence. Such violence not only occurs within the family, but it has penetrated homes for the aged, where the latter may be abused by the personnel. Some research on the violence done to old people, both in the home and in institutions, is being initiated, but there have been very few such studies to date. However, sooner or later the acuteness of the problem will force policy makers to pay much more attention to this aspect of aging.

In the United States, it is estimated (Steinmetz 1981) that about 10% of persons 65 and over are vulnerable and stand a very good chance of being maltreated by the persons on whom they depend for their needs and their care. According to King (1984), American estimates in 1981 of the number of old people who were victims of this type of violence varied form 500,000 to a million every year. In Canada, the Department of Health and Welfare estimates that 100,000 elderly persons are abused (Radio Canada: "Le Point" 1986). The number of cases known or reported is probably much lower than the actual number, however, because the victims often remain silent, fearing reprisals on the one hand, and on the other, being reluctant to inform on their own children. Dependent, feeble and beset by all sorts of mixed feelings, of which maternal or paternal love is not the least, they rarely lodge a complaint against their child, especially since in many cases, the abuse is difficult to describe or document.

Furthermore, according to projections, the number of victims is expected to increase considerably with the years. In an American survey by Shanas (1979), the data seem to indicate that more and more families will take care of parents for a long time rather than place them in institutions. Studies lead to the conclusion that inflation will cause an even greater number of aged persons to live with members of their family. More vulnerable old people will then be exposed to abusive treatment. Without an increase in assistance to families and without more protective organizations, abuses can become still more widespread.

NEGLECT AND ABUSE: TOWARD A DEFINITION

In their study of the elderly abuse in Massachusetts, O'Malley *et al.* (1984) use the term "elder abuse and neglect" to cover all situations in which elderly persons are subjected to blows, rudeness, verbal violence, negation of their rights, neglect in the administration of the care necessary, infantilization, desertion or a poor use of available resources. The authors define abuse and neglect as follows:

> ABUSE: Active intervention by a caregiver such that unmet needs are created or sustained with resultant physical, psychological or financial injury;
> NEGLECT: Failure of a caregiver to intervene to resolve a significant care need despite awareness of available resources (p. 362).

Based on the results of research in Manitoba, Shell (1982) observes that, according to the persons questioned, in the majority of cases, the abuses perpetrated on the elderly were not intentional. In the respondents' view, these unintentional abuses most often were the result of events that were beyond the control of the persons in charge (whether a relative or not). Because of this, they were incapable of lavishing the care necessary or controlling moods that could be prejudicial to their charges. Having said this, in order to prevent the concepts of "neglect" and "abuse" from becoming too broad, it is necessary to restrict them, as Costa (1984) does, to cruelty that is intentional. Shell's definition refers only to acts and behaviour that are conscious: "The willful infliction of physical pain, injury, or debilitating mental anguish, unreasonable confinement or willful deprivation by a caregiver of services that are necessary to maintain mental and physical health" (p. 58). Other researchers (Hickey and Douglass 1981a) differentiate between *passive* neglect, not looking after the elderly person (leaving the person alone, isolated, or making him or her wait unduly) and *active* neglect (withholding necessities of daily life such as food, medicines, company and the assistance needed for hygienic and other reasons).

In a study in Quebec by Bélanger *et al.* (1981) on abuses in the institutional and family milieus, the authors — inspired by the work of Block and Sinnot in Maryland (1979) — described five forms of violence to which the elderly are subjected: (1) *physical abuse* — inadequate food; diet not adhered to; medical instructions not followed; willfully inflicted injuries; tying the victim to the bed or to a chair; grievous assault, rape, murder; (2) *psychological abuse* — verbal assault; threats; blackmail; abuse of authority; illegal confinement; abandonment by the family; depreciation of the individual; (3) *material abuse* (theft of money, pension cheques, jewelry, handbag; fraud, exorbitant rent, etc.); (4) *violation of rights and freedoms* — eviction from home; forced institutionalization; limitation of visiting hours; medicines or prostheses not furnished; forced medication, etc.; and (5) *conditions of the environment* — inadequate heating; fire hazard; prohibition against personalizing the surroundings and keeping personal objects.

On the other hand, Yin (1985) finds that the term "abuse" is used much too broadly and that, taken to the extreme, it can include all forms of conflict that can arise in personal relationships. In his opinion, psychological abuse could be extended to anything that frustrates an elderly person. The same is true of violation of an old person's rights. Apart from attempts on the integrity of his person or his goods, this author finds it difficult to think of individual rights whose violation is serious enough to be considered an "abuse". In Yin's definition, then, he refers only to *"financial* abuse" and *"physical* abuse".

Yin defines the former as all types of crime against the property of an elderly person by the members of his family or someone he trusts. This includes all forms of larceny, fraud, theft and automobile theft. As for "physical abuse", he defines it as the intentional use of force or an act of willful — not accidental — omission on the part of a relative or caregiver, for the purpose of upsetting, injuring or destroying the elderly person. In fact, Yin's approach is "criminological" and contrasts with the "gerontological" approach of many American researchers such as Brock (1980), Hickey and Douglass (1981), Lau and Kosberg (1979) and many others who feel that considering the advanced age of the victims (80 or more, for the most part), a moral or psychological wrong has considerable influence on their mental and physical health. The aged are a particularly vulnerable group, and it is for this reason that behaviour which is not a "crime", strictly speaking, but constitutes a senseless act of cruelty, should not be excluded from studies on the abuse of old people.

A general definition of abuse, then, would be *any act or intentional omission that causes old people physical suffering, serious psychological disturbance, undue violation of their rights and freedoms or any attack against their person or property*. In fact, we consider abuse any act or intentional omission that the oppressor knows in advance will cause the elderly person serious physical or mental suffering.

THE CAUSES OF ABUSE

In the United States, in 1981, only 5.3% of the elderly lived in nursing homes. Studies have shown unequivocally that the greatest source of abuse is the family. There is no reason to think the situation is any different in Canada even though a few more elderly people live in institutions.[1] In 1981, 6.5% of males and 10.5% of females 65 and over were living in Canadian collective households (Statistics Canada 1984). This situation could slightly increase the opportunity for abuse by non-family members. To understand the causes of abuse, it it important to describe the findings of major studies done in this domain (King 1984). The profile of the victims that emerges is that they are mostly women 75 years of age and over; most suffer from physical or mental deterioration; they live with their aggressor on whom they are physically, mentally and financially dependent. Based on her Manitoba study, Shell (1982) states that older people who are abused are for the most part women between 80 and 84 who have been living with a member of their family for 10 years or more. O'Malley and his collaborators (1979) have found that the victims, in 75% of cases, live with their oppressor; the latter, moreover, is most often (84%) a relative. This being the case, it becomes obvious that in order to understand the complex, often ambiguous ties that bind the aggressor and the victim, the social, family and individual factors that might explain the genesis of the abuse must be looked into.

Societal Factors

There are a number of social factors that provide a first explanation for the increase in cases of "elderly abuse": (1) the disappearance of the extended family and its replacement by the nuclear family; (2) an aging population with increased longevity due to medical science; (3) the more widespread use of violence and brutality at all levels of society and (4) a devaluation, in industrial cultures, of the experience and wisdom that had for a long time been prerogatives associated with advancing age. Chen *et al.* (1981) believe that the sub-culture of violence that characterizes some segments of the American society may also contribute to the rising incidence of abuse of the elderly.

To this, as Katz (1979–80) points out, must be added the general attitude of the population toward the aged — a factor that contributes to the emergence of abuses. It is ageism, which Butler (1975) describes, in its simplest form, as *"just not wanting to have all those ugly old people around"* (p. 35). Kahana *et al.* (1977) describe it as a discriminatory attitude toward the elderly, one that is adopted by social agencies, organizations, groups and individuals. According to the authors, this prejudice against the elderly includes job discrimination (obligatory retirement at 65), rejection by certain organizations (insurance companies, for example), problems with government agencies (regarding taxes, old age pensions, etc.), the indifference of the police to their requests or complaints and ill-treatment at the hands of their families.

Family Factors

In Michigan, Hickey and Douglass (1981a) are convinced that in families where the oldest members are abused, it is a manifestation of resentment against having the burden of caring for an old person. Perhaps the "me first" reaction has become more prevalent in the last few years. At the same time, many relatives are simply not capable of taking adequate care of aged and extremely dependent members of their family. For instance, women in the labour force have less time, less energy and interest to care for an older parent. The result of this, as Chen *et al.* (1981) believe, is that aged parents sometimes serve as scapegoats or as targets for the release of tensions caused by other problems besetting the children or relatives on whom they are dependent.

Crowded conditions generally, and particularly in housing, insufficient incomes, conjugal problems, alcohol abuse and the numerous complications and tensions arising from the dependence of older members of the family on the youngest are also elements that can lead to abusive treatment. More specifically, the research shows consistently that abusive adults were themselves victims of maltreatment when they were children (Hickey and Douglass 1981a; Shell 1982). There seems to be a "boomerang" effect, a cyclic process whereby the older members of the family, in their turn, are abused.

Individual Factors

Other factors that explain the abuse of old people sometimes stem from the victims themselves. Some old people deliberately shift all responsibility onto the shoulders of others. They give up all autonomy; they no longer want to run their own lives. Thus, they become an even heavier burden on those responsible for them, since they expect to be taken in hand without making any effort to help themselves or simplify the task of the persons looking after them.

Moreover, as Katz (1979–80) points out, a large part of the problem of abuse comes from the economic, physical and emotional difficulties of living with dependent persons: "When the difficulty of caring for someone who may be infirm, incontinent or incapable is compounded by a lack of closeness or troubled relationship in the past or by stressful changes in the lives of adult children, the resulting stress and frustration may create a potential of violence" (p. 701). It is very often, then, in a disturbed family milieu that violence occurs.

The conclusions of Hickey and Douglass (1981b), as well as those of Steinmetz (1978), lead one to think that the sudden and unwanted dependence of a relative may evoke negative or even malicious behaviour in the members of a family. This is even more probable if the elderly person is at the mercy of others for his vital needs. The dependent person, because of his or her "intrusion" in a closed family circle, can therefore be a source of tension emotionally, physically and financially for the adult children, who are often ill-prepared to assume the responsibility of an aged parent, or are incapable of taking proper care of him or her. According to Anderson (1981), the health of the elderly person and the attitude of the "caregivers" toward aging are factors that weigh equally in influencing the quality of the relationship and the onset of maltreatment. They can also trigger an escalation of violence, notes the same author, should the reaction of the elderly victim take the form of resignation, withdrawal, fear, depression or mental confusion.

Important too, is the fact that the elderly live in extreme insecurity. Many of them have seen their mates, their parents and their friends die. They consequently feel very much alone. They feel they are useless, unproductive and have no status in the family. Little by little, many lose their mobility and their independence, thus restricting their contacts with friends and contemporaries more and more. These losses imperceptibly create a feeling of rejection and hopelessness that leads to passivity and subordination. At the same time, their attitudes and behaviour often change, not only due to the aging process, but also as a result of chronic illnesses, such as diabetes, strokes, blindness, deafness, arthritis or heart attacks. In addition, sometimes certain medicines or a combination of medicines may result in personality changes. This may partially explain the appearance of some of the character traits in elderly people described by Bertrand (1980): distrust, egocentricity, shamelessness and tyranny.

In the end, some elderly persons become a difficult burden for those around them: "Even the most devoted and responsible caregiver may see feelings of love and respect erode into anger, guilt, and disappointment after years of tiring caregiving" (King 1984, 9). As a result it may be more and more difficult to establish a suitable haven for the aged. The final irony no doubt is that it will be the youth of today who tomorrow may find themselves victims of their own indifference to the problem of aging. As expressed so well by Simone de Beauvoir, life would have us refuse to recognize ourselves in the old person we will become.

DYNAMICS OF THE RELATIONSHIP BETWEEN AGGRESSOR AND VICTIM

Studies by Rathbone-McCuan (1980) show that old people who are mal-treated are generally functionally dependent, either because of insufficient financial resources or because of mental or physical disabilities. A study by O'Malley *et al.* (1979) concludes that in 75% of the cases of abuse, the victim was mentally or physically handicapped. If we now consider the two poles of interaction between victim and oppressor, it is interesting to note the results of Steinmetz' research (1983) on "reciprocal" violence: one percent of the adults questioned admitted having had recourse to acts of violence in dealing with an aged parent, whereas 18% answered that it was the latter who had used physical violence against them.

Moreover, as Rifai (1977) points out, aging not only has physiological and psychic implications, it is accompanied by a loss of social esteem, a lessening of self-confidence, diminished economic security and little emotional support. Old people thus become vulnerable. For some relatives or caregivers, they become ideal targets for their hostility, their frustrations and their contempt. A poor state of health, increasing their dependence, can accentuate the caregiver's resentment. Other factors come into play as well. Research indicates that many members of a family who look after an aged parent are getting on in years themselves. Anderson (1981) points out a study where 75% of the subjects who were caring for a parent were more than 50 years of age, and 20% of them were even over 70. Steinmetz (1981), in her research, found that 57% of caregivers were retired with fixed incomes and also had health problems.

Taking care of an elderly person often creates stress, which is the source of most cases of abuse. King (1984) notes that among adults who took care of a parent at home, 40% devoted the equivalent of a full-time job to it. It is indeed a full-time job, thankless and trying, and requires nerves of steel, affection, and a great deal of control in order not to sometimes show exasperation and irritation. Other studies, among them that of Anderson (1981), show that adults in charge of elders can experience feelings of deprivation or depression because of the heavy responsibility they have inherited when they finally find themselves free of their children's upbringing.

Just as they were beginning to see their retirement as a period of freedom and relaxation in which they would be able to enjoy their financial independence, they now have to assume charge of an aged parent, involving not only the cost of food and shelter but the cost of the care required as well. It also represents a cost in terms of time and loss of freedom; this situation may easily engender conflicts between aged parents and their children who never expected to play this role. "The children may have unarticulated feelings that the parent's financial problems should be ignored, or even openly stated feelings that the parent's time is past and that the offspring's financial resources should be spent on the advancement of their own families" (Katz 1979–80, 701). On the other hand, the aged parent can be disappointed in his own expectations of comfort and freedom at this period of his life, which he envisioned as a time of tranquility, rest and security. Faced with reality, he may let himself go, lose all initiative and depend more and more on those who have assumed his care.

STUDIES ON ABUSE OF THE ELDERLY

There has been research for several years now on the abuse of old people, both within the family context and in the institutional milieu. However, most of it has concentrated more on family violence, for it is within the family that abuses most often occur. We have already mentioned, in fact, that only a small percentage of old people, around 8% in Canada, are admitted to institutions. A brief discussion follows on the methods used in this research and the results regarding the oppressors, the types of abusive behaviour and their consequences.

Methodology

Before reporting the results of the research in this domain, it seems important to describe the enormous methodological difficulties such studies involve. They most often concern hidden abuse that is not reported. It is quite obvious that attacks on the property and integrity of a person that occur in a situation where oppressor and victim know one another and live under the same roof can only be committed with impunity against helpless and vulnerable individuals, who are unable to defend themselves or lodge a complaint. The proof is that the old people who are abused are, in the majority of cases, over 70 years of age, even 80 and over, and suffer from physical and mental deterioration that leaves them tied hand and foot to their aggressor. This fact makes surveys on the abuse and ill-treatment of the elderly extremely difficult. Sometimes these old people are unable to give information for fear of reprisals on the part of the family or the hospital personnel in charge of them, or again because they no longer have the necessary mental clarity to be able to answer a questionnaire.

In view of the difficulty of doing a direct survey of the target population, researchers have tried to analyze elder abuse by indirect means. Two methods were adopted. The most widely used consists in getting evidence from people — doctors, nurses, social workers and other caregivers — who are in direct contact with elderly persons, concerning the types and frequency of the abuses to which old people are subjected. This type of research is mostly carried out among professionals and volunteers working with families. Because of the difficulties involved, few studies have been done on the maltreatment of old people in public institutions.

The second method, used much less often, consists in talking to adults who have charge of an elderly parent, with a view to examining the types of behaviour they adopt toward their aged parents. Relying on the frankness of the persons questioned, it is a matter of discovering whether or not acts of violence or financial exploitation have occurred. Yin (1985) is of the opinion that this is a good method that has proved successful in the case of violence against children and between husband and wife (Gil 1970 and Strauss *et al.* 1980). Furthermore, he believes there should be recourse to direct surveys of the aged persons themselves, apart from those living in old peoples' homes, of course, for they are very old and most of them mentally impaired. Whatever the case, in spite of all the research done to date, it has been impossible to get precise data on the extent and gravity of the abuse of elderly persons, for most of these abuses are hidden behind the "closed doors" of family homes. Nonetheless, these studies, for the most part exploratory and descriptive, enable us to define the nature of the problem and certain characteristics of it.

Visibility

The abuses to which the elderly are subjected are rarely visible because they are most often practised within the family, far from the view of outsiders. Even in public or para-public institutions they often escape the attention of persons who could report or put a stop to them. In the United States, a study completed by Stannard (1973) in a nursing home for old people showed that the nurses were not aware that patients were being abused. Those in closest contact with the older persons and for the longest periods of time, the orderlies and nurses' aids, were those most likely to tyrannize the patients in order to control them more easily. Stannard defined abusive behaviour in the institutional milieu as any act which, known to a nurse, would be punished; for example, hitting or tying up a patient, or terrorizing a patient by actions or threats.

Stannard's research is particularly interesting as the author gathered his data by means of intensive participant observation that took place over a period of nearly a year. He concludes that most abuses are not seen by professional personnel. This indicates that the results of research based on interviewing qualified caregivers pertain only to the abusive behaviour they have witnessed, which is far from the reality.

Abuse in Institutions

The fate of elderly persons in institutions for the aged has been drawing the attention of researchers for some years now. In Canada, as we have said, it is estimated that about 7% of the population over 65 live in homes or community residences reserved for senior citizens. Studies of these institutions note cases of abuse or negligence (some of them criminal), maltreatment (both physical and psychological), and in general a cold and dehumanizing atmosphere (Hahn 1976; Hacker 1977; Bélanger *et al.* 1981). Two sociologists at the University of Toronto, who did a three-year study on the quality of life in old people's homes, report that elderly residents lose their autonomy and even their personality. According to Carolyn Singer and Lilian Wells (Creighton 1986: p. k. 7), there is a tendency in these institutions to treat the residents like children rather than adults: "the problem is even more deeply rooted in that the old people are rewarded for their quiescence. If they try to question the system they are considered problem cases". The researchers further state that the main complaints of the people living in institutions are the lack of privacy, the poor quality of the food and the treatment they suffer at the hands of certain members of the personnel. Their study showed that the residents, contrary to the employees, are of the opinion that physical comfort is not a priority in these establishments. They feel the accent should be on personal development. According to the authors, efforts should be redoubled to maintain and increase the autonomy and potential of the elderly living in institutions rather than treating them like children and reducing them to brutish passivity, which finally robs them of whatever self-esteem they may have had.

Another phenomenon that is now beginning to be considered criminal is the "battered parents" syndrome, whether perpetrated by the children or by near relatives responsible for their care (Smith 1979; Shell 1982). This syndrome comprises acts of physical assault, abandonment, neglect and financial exploitation, and the situation is all the more serious in that elderly victims remain silent about them.

Obviously, the situation of a victim of physical cruelty at the hands of a member of his family is delicate. The victim hesitates to complain, it seems, because a precarious balance of dependency has been established between the two. A woman, beaten by her son, for example, will not denounce him because he is the sole guarantee that she will maintain her autonomy and remain at home. If she should denounce him, it would mean institutionalization or at least removal from his care and giving up a way of life she is anxious to maintain.

It is estimated that, in Canada (Radio Canada: Le Point 1986), more than 100,000 senior citizens'[2]; the majority of them women, are subjected to physical, psychological and financial abuse each year. The persons responsible, moreover, are not necessarily employees of homes for the aged, but are frequently the children of those abused. According to William Corns, however, 100,000 is a "very modest" figure because the elderly are often afraid to report cases of abuse (*The Globe and Mail Toronto*; A 11). Since the establishment in Toronto of Mayor Arthur Eggleton's "Committee on Aging", numerous cases of abuse have come to light. The members of the Committee found cases of physical abuse, of people not getting proper food, of their pension cheques being taken away from them, and their being forced to sign over their property and then put in a home where the children never visit them. However, these cases need to be better documented. The fact remains that we are dealing here with a hidden problem which is only beginning to surface. The Committee has published a brochure entitled "Elder Abuse", in which four types are described: *physical* abuse, in which the victims are beaten and subjected to various forms of maltreatment; *psychological*, in which the elderly are treated like children, scolded, called names and denied access to their friends and grandchildren; *financial*, in which they are forced to sign over control of their assets; and *neglect*, which often means being confined to a room, without proper food, medical attention or personal care.

In a large number of cases, senior citizens are obliged to make enormous changes in their way of life when forced to enter an institution. Often the elderly person is allowed no part in the decision to move, at a certain point being considered unable to look after himself or make his own decisions. Institutionalization very often concretizes an isolation and rejection that had already begun. As for the living conditions in homes for the aged, although abuses were not very visible and were hard to detect, researchers were able, nonetheless, to report cases of physical violence. Oddly enough, this physical violence was not only inflicted by the personnel, as one would be inclined to think, but sometimes occurred between the residents themselves as well. For example, a resident who would like to have a room alone would systematically be cruel to his or her room-mate in order to force the latter to leave. More often than not, it is consequently the confused and helpless who are attacked.

A study in Quebec (Bélanger *et al.* 1981), on a population of 140 professionals (nurses, social workers, administrators, community workers, home care assistants) shows that 7% had never heard of abusive treatment of old people; that 36% had heard about it but did not know any specific cases; and finally that 57% knew of at least one case of maltreatment. Yet all of them worked in the social services, in homes or in hospitals directly involved in the care of older people. It might have been expected, therefore, that they would all know of at least one case where an older person had been abused. All the more so, since the author's definition was very broad, including physical, psychological and financial abuse as well as the violation of rights and denial of many of the comforts of life. When these five forms of violence were analyzed according to the percentage of respondents who had witnessed them or known about them, the results were as follows:

— 34% of the respondents reported psychological abuse. In order of importance, it was verbal assault (41%); abandonment by the family (40%); threats or blackmail (37%); denegration of the person (37%); abuse of authority (37%) and isolation (11%);

— 30% of the professionals questioned mentioned material abuses, either the theft of money or pension cheques (36%) or theft of personal objects, especially jewelry and handbags (32%); the imposition of exorbitant rents (28%) or swindling (26%);

— 25% of the persons interviewed mentioned physical abuse: inadequate food or diet not followed (35%); medical care not maintained (31%); injuries deliberately inflicted (24%); person tied to the bed, to a chair (24%); grievous assault such as rape or murder (12%);

— 25% of them had witnessed or had known of poor environmental conditions: of these, there was inadequate heating, risk of fire, etc. (31%); not allowing personal effects to be kept (24%); not allowing personalizing of the surroundings (21%);

— 23% reported violations of the rights of old people: forced institutionalization (38%); eviction from the home (28%); obligation to take unnecessary medication; restrictions limiting visiting hours (15%); and finally, not furnishing medicines or prostheses indispensable to the patients' welfare (15%).

This Montreal study has the advantage of having surveyed caregivers who were able to observe acts of violence in both public institutions and in families. Unfortunately, the analysis does not give the distribution of the types of abusive conduct according to their place of origin — the family, public institutions, hospitals, unauthorized homes or residential centres. We do know, however, that 35.5% of the abusive behaviour was observed in public institutions (residential centres, hospitals, etc.); that 26% were in the elderly person's own home (21.6%) and in that of a relative (4.4%); that 28.4% of the acts of violence known to professionals took place in unauthorized homes, that is, non-subsidized foster homes (12.7%), in private institutions receiving government aid (12.1%) and in foster families (3.6%). The remaining abusive behaviour that was seen or reported took place in rooms, boarding houses, in the street or in public places.

Of the 974 acts of abuse known to or witnessed by the 140 subjects surveyed, 43.1% were perpetrated by members of the personnel of public institutions; 23.5% by relatives (children, daughters-in-law or sons-in-law, mates or other relatives), 19.1% by strangers (landlords, janitors, unknown persons) and 14.3% by persons taking charge of old people (personnel of private institutions, persons assuming charge of the elderly). The research shows that old people are subjected to violence in every milieu. If the frequency of cases of maltreatment seems to be relatively higher in nursing homes and hospitals than in families, we believe there are two reasons for this: (a) the professionals surveyed were working in institutions, for the most part, and (b) abusive treatment is perhaps more visible in the institutional context (although, as Stannard (1973) shows, visibility there too is very poor), than within the family circle, which is much more closed and impenetrable. Furthermore, most old people live with their family, which explains why research has concentrated on domestic violence to aged parents.

Domestic Violence

Based on surveys among the social services and among professionals, as well as on police statistics, it turns out that their own relatives are the main source of the maltreatment of old people. Lau and Kosberg (1979) analyzed the files of all persons 60 and over who had been treated during the course of one year at the Chronic Illness Center of Cleveland, Ohio. Of 404 cases, 39 — or 9.6% — had been the victims of abuse at the hands of their family. Among the victims, 74% had suffered physical violence (for two-thirds it took the form of neglect and lack of personal care, and for the rest, direct beating); 51% suffered from psychological violence (verbal assault, threats); 31% had been subjected to material abuse (theft, misappropriation of money and goods) and 18% to infringement of their rights (ejection from their residence or home; forcible placement in an institution). These figures bear witness to the extent of abuses to which the elderly fall victim; Eastman and Sutton (1982) estimated at 42% of the number of persons 65 and over, in the United States, who were in the care of relatives and at 10% of the number of these who were victims of violence.

Family violence is hard to study. Most authors who have studied it have proceeded in an indirect way by conducting surveys among professionals. These are the most likely to witness any violence, either because they are called upon to make visits to the home, or because in the hospitals and social agencies they are used to receiving old people who are the victims of cruelty or maltreatment. An attempt was made to evaluate the extent of abuse based on the knowledge of professionals working with the aged (doctors, nurses, social workers, home care assistants). O'Malley *et al.* (1979), in their study in Massachusetts, reported that, over a period of 18 months, 55% of their respondents (N = 183/332) had known of cases of elder abuse. In Maryland, Block and Sinnott (1979) observed in their survey that

13.4% of the persons questioned who were working with old people had witnessed at least one case of maltreatment. In Michigan, Hickey and Douglass (1981a, 1981b), in turn, noted that of a population of 228 professionals, 60% said they handled cases of abuse regularly in their work.

Aside from the study done by Lau and Kosberg, already cited, and which dealt with a clientele that had been treated in hospital, in most research that has been conducted, the same conclusion has been arrived at, namely, that there is much less physical violence than other forms of violence or abuse. The relative proportions of the diverse types of violence vary according to the regions studied, the professional categories questioned, the methods used and the definitions given to the different forms of abuse.

Some Canadian Data on Family Violence Toward the Elderly

A study similar to the American surveys of professionals and paraprofessionals was done by Shell (1982) in Manitoba. Her survey focussed on doctors, police officers, lawyers, members of the clergy and, above all, nurses (working either in home care programs or in hospitals). In all, there were semi-structured interviews with 105 persons, who declared that, over the course of one year, they had known of 402 cases of abuse. When an old person had suffered several forms of violence, each one was counted separately. Thus, Shell registered 540 abuses in all, involving 402 persons 60 and over. According to type, they were distributed as follows:

— 40.3% (N = 217) material abuse: half of these (50.4%) involved the cashing of pension or social security cheques; the rest were fraud (19.2%), theft (15.6%), exorbitantly high rents (6.7%), excessive payment demanded for services rendered (4.9%) and misappropriation of goods (3.1%);

— 37.5% (N = 202) psycho-social violence: humiliation, intimidation, infantilization (38.6%); insufficient or total lack of attention for long periods (17.5%); isolation (13.9%); exclusion from active participation in the person's own destiny (11.2%); confinement (7.2%); threats of violence (6.8%); threats of abandonment or placement in an institution (4.8%);

— 22.5% (N = 121) physical violence: assault and battery (35.1%); malnutrition (11.7%); harsh treatment (11%); negligence of proper hygiene (11%); lack of medical care (7.8%); excessive medication (5.2%); sexual aggression (4.5%); homicide (3.9%); restraint (2.6%); willful negligence causing accidents (1.9%).

Concerning the perpetrators of this abuse, 24.4% were practitioners having no connection with the victim, whereas 75.6% were members of the family. Of the latter, 60% were men, and 40% women. In order of percentages, it was the son or son-in-law (23.6%), the daughter or daughter-in-law (21.2%), the husband (16.4%), the wife (3.7%) and other relatives (6.1%).

Among the victims there were twice as many women (68%) as men (32%), and in 70% of the cases, they were over 70 years of age.

In Massachusetts, O'Malley *et al.* (1984) arrived at similar figures: 72% of abused parents were 70 and over. Based on their study, they established that 86% of the abusers were relatives, that 75% were living with the victim and that many of them were under stress, had alcohol or drug problems, had been ill for a long time or were in financial difficulties. The people questioned by Shell confirmed almost the same facts. Alcoholism was considered a high risk factor for potential maltreatment by 44.8% of the Canadian respondents; tensions over finances by 15.2%; a bad attitude toward aging by 10.5%; inability to adapt and to react emotionally by 8.6%; the fact of being old (60 and over) by 5.7% and mental instability by 5.7% as well.

Lamont (1985), who had carried out in-depth interviews with six people working with the elderly in Quebec, gathered testimony on about 30 cases of serious abuse of old people. In order to describe the actual interactions between victim and oppressor, brief resumés of four case histories were made from this study as follows:

— Madame A had her pension cheque taken from her regularly by an alcoholic son. Furthermore, when he was drunk, he would hit her. With almost no resources, she could barely feed herself and look after her needs. She had to be placed in a home in order to be protected from the son.

— Madame D, 75 years old, asked her niece to take her in. The latter tried to get rid of her. She insulted her. She frequently abused her. Sometimes she even doused her with water. She finally beat her, and stabbed her with a screwdriver.

— An elderly couple was manipulated by a son who had no resources and had to find money to pay his rent, buy food and look after his personal expenses. By threatening his parents, he got everything he wanted out of them. He entered their home without warning. He stripped them of their belongings, and stole whatever he wanted.

— Madame K lived alone. A nephew came to do light work and some messages for her. Little by little, the nephew became more and more demanding and more aggressive. One day when he was on drugs, he beat her, hit her with a hammer and raped her.

These examples show that the very vulnerability of old people, and women in this case, triggers aggression and violence on the part of relatives and family, who live in stressful situations themselves. These cases graphically illustrate the data presented by O'Malley *et al.* and by Shell, cited earlier.

Incidentally, based on information that was obtained from the various professionals questioned, Shell was able to ascertain that more than a third of the oppressors (36.6%) were over 60. Steinmetz (1983) confirms the fact that, more and more, the caregivers are themselves advanced in age. Her research shows that the average age of the adults looking after aged parents was 48. More than 60% of them were 55 and over. As Shell (1982) noted in her research in Manitoba:

> A large number of abusive caregivers were found to be over 60 years of age. This is in accord with previous research findings suggesting that many caregivers are themselves likely to be elderly. This suggests that the responsibility of caring for a dependent elderly person, together with the caregiver's own status — retirement, fixed income, increased health problems — combine to produce a breaking point and a situation conducive to abuse (p. 44).

In general, the American studies (Block and Sinnott 1979: Lau and Kosberg 1979; Steuer and Austin 1980) showed that the people with the highest risk of victimization were very old women, severely deteriorated physically and mentally, who were dependent on a relative for their care and support. This is because physical and psychological dependency stimulates aggression and "oppression/oppressed" relationships. The care of a submissive (helpless) person 24 hours a day, according to O'Rourke (1981), almost always provokes fatigue, exhaustion, nervousness and illness that can generate acts of violence. Furthermore, as Lau and Kosberg note (1979), taking in an aged parent upsets the family routine, changes family relationships and interactions, limits the freedom of each of its members, and consequently is a source of stress and conflict.

UNDERSTANDING AND HELPING THE ELDERLY

Given the results of the various studies on the abuse of old people, and in view of the continual increase in the number of persons 65 and over, there is a possible danger that violence toward aged parents will take on even greater and more dramatic proportions. It would be well for the Canadian Government to adopt measures as soon as possible to prevent this from happening. A law should be passed for "the protection of the elderly". This law would govern the responsibilities of "caregivers", would define the recourse open to old people who are wronged and would create services to prevent and combat violence. This law, as Bélanger *et al.* (1981) suggest, should see to the integration of older people in society while ensuring them specific means of protection. "The accent should be on encouragement more than coercion, since it is true that violence against the elderly is as much a question of changing mentalities as it is of suppressing behaviour" (p. 37). Above all, young people have to be aware that the way they treat their elders to a certain extent defines the way they will be treated when they are old.

Also, as O'Rourke (1981) suggests, the contribution of families that take care of their aged parents must be recognized and they must be given essential services to help them in their task: home care, meals-on-wheels, nursing services, day centres, relief and consultation resources. Considering the fact that stress, alcoholism, drug consumption and illness are causes of abusive behaviour, "counselling" must be offered both aggressor and victim, in order, when possible, to get them to resolve their problems and control their aggression.

CONCLUSION

In 1981, in Canada, 6.7% of persons 65 and over and 33% of those 85 and over were living in nursing homes and institutions for the elderly and chronically ill (Chappell *et al.* 1986). These percentages are expected to increase, for demographic estimates show that by the year 2031, there will be 7,128,400 persons 65 and over, representing 23.9% of the Canadian population compared with 10% today (Statistics Canada 1984). The proportion of old people in our society is growing rapidly and we can expect that it will require a larger number of families and institutions to see to their needs. This will necessarily influence the number of cases of abuse and maltreatment, which, based on the cases known today, should increase from 100,000 to at least 250,000 cases a year. If nothing is done before then, the situation will be catastrophic.

Research, undertaken by Shell for the Manitoba Council on Aging (1982), measured the amount of elderly abuse: "It is clear", she writes, "that we are faced with a problem of considerable dimension and seriousness" (p. 44). The problem is even more serious in that the victims are among the oldest and most vulnerable of our senior citizens; this is particularly true of women from 80 to 84 years of age, living with a member of their family for the past ten years or more. Since more elderly people live with their family than in institutions, it is within the family that there is the greatest risk of abuse. The fact is that, with improved living conditions and the strides made in medicine, more people are now living to an advanced age. This increase in the aged population is exerting pressure on institutions for the chronically ill and on the social services which are unable to take care of all the elderly, and which are trying to keep the most self-reliant at home with their family. More and more families are being encouraged to assume their responsibility toward their elders.

According to Shell (1982), the maltreatment of the elderly through negligence or brutality is not inconsiderable. The research cited in this chapter demonstrates that cases of abuse and maltreatment are not the exception. These studies justify any fears people may have about the magnitude of the problem concerning senior citizens and their families and the personnel in institutions. The findings of researchers, therefore, should encourage policy makers to put forward programs to improve the quality of life for the elderly. There should be special services for senior citizens, for example, assistance to families that are taking care of an older person, information, financial support, day centres, temporary lodging facilities, assistance to those at home. A system of emergency intervention should also be developed because it is often during a family crisis that situations occur that provoke acts of violence and abuse. In the institutions, moreover, the personnel should be trained and supervised in order to avoid the frustrations, the discontent and consequent aggression that can occur on the part of the nurses and attendants who look after older persons. In short, it is essential to promote the rights of senior citizens and to make the rest of the population aware of their contribution to society, their role and their expectations, in order to change the attitude of the population — an attitude that is too often negative — toward the elderly.

NOTES

1. In Canada, the definition of institutional care includes nursing homes and institutions for the elderly and chronically ill. The figure for the United States includes nursing homes only. Personal care homes and domicillary care are not included in the definition of nursing homes (Chappell, Strain and Blandford 1986).
2. This figure of 100,000 elderly victims of abuse was based on the evaluations of various senior citizen groups across the country.

CHAPTER 7

RESEARCH AND SOCIAL POLICIES

There has been very little research in Canada to date on the violent and criminal acts perpetrated against the elderly, yet this type of crime has become an urgent social problem. With the rapid demographic changes in the country, in scarcely more than 20 years from now, one in five persons will be 65 years of age and over. There is a compelling need, therefore, to undertake research on the domestic and social violence perpetrated against older Canadians as well as on their criminal victimization. This would make it possible, on the basis of objective data, to set up programs and measures ensuring the elderly security and a better quality of life.

RÉSUMÉ OF THE RESEARCH DATA

Because of their special vulnerability, the elderly should be considered a specific group of victims. Only by studying the victimization of people over 60 and their style of life and socio-economic conditions, can we develop preventive measures and social policies that will answer their needs. In spite of the fact that elderly people do not form a homogeneous group, they have a number of characteristics in common that make them the subject of particular study.

Criminological research has shown that a number of traits distinguish the aged from other members of the population as far as victimization, fear of crime and their attitudes toward crime and criminal justice are concerned. The principal conclusions and data available at the present time are presented in the following pages.

Age and Vulnerability

The aging process is one of increasing physical weakness that makes old people an "easy" target for criminals. There are many people 65 and over, particularly women, who are incapable of running away or defending themselves against an aggressor. Yet, surveys show that in spite of this weakness, the elderly are victims of crime, especially violent crime, less often than younger people, whose style of life exposes them more to this type of victimization. In Canada, in the seven largest urban centres, senior citizens — who represented 9.7% of the population in 1981 — were victims of fewer than 2% of all personal attacks. Incidents of a violent and personal nature amounted to only about a sixth of all the crimes committed against the senior citizens surveyed (Solicitor General of Canada 1985: Bulletin No. 6). Furthermore, when the statistics are compiled according to types of criminal attack, they show that in the case of certain offences, senior citizens are being victimized at a rate that is totally out of proportion to the rest of the population. This is the case, for example, for pocket picking or purse snatching, burglary, robbery, confidence games and deceptive practices (Corrigan 1981).

The Consequences of Victimization

Although the elderly are generally victims of less serious crimes, or at least it appears so, the consequences of these acts are much more traumatic for this age group than for any other. This is confirmed by the Canadian Urban Victimization Survey (Solicitor General of Canada 1983, 1984, 1985). According to this study, however, there is a greater chance of senior citizens being victims of serious crimes than other age groups, that is to say, the proportion for this age group is higher than for others:

> The relatively low rates of crime against elderly people should not lead us to minimize the problem. When elderly people were victimized they were more likely than other age groups to be seriously victimized. The ratio of more serious to less serious crimes was higher among the elderly than among younger people. The ratio of robberies to personal thefts, for example, was 30 to 100 among the elderly and only 15 to 100 among other age groups (Solicitor General of Canada 1985c, Bulletin No. 6, 2).

For Hahn (1976), there is no doubt that the elderly are special victims for whom the consequences of a crime are much worse than for other citizens. Moreover, the Canadian survey shows that although elderly victims were no more likely than younger ones to have suffered injuries, the consequences of their injuries were generally more serious. For example, "elderly victims who were injured were twice as likely as younger victims to have required medical and dental attention" (Solicitor General 1985, 2). The physical frailty of persons 65 and over makes the consequences of an attack more hazardous.

The same study indicated that for the Canadian sample, the financial repercussions of victimization were also more serious for senior citizens than for others. Because of their relatively low annual incomes, the losses sustained by elderly victims, in terms of percentage of their income, were twice as high as they were for victims from 25 to 64, and three and a half times higher than those of victims from 16 to 24.

Conditions of Life and Fear of Crime

A number of studies stress the difficult conditions of life experienced by some senior citizens. Many have a low income, not indexed to the cost of living. This results in gradually increasing proverty as the years go by. Thus, many live in low rental neighbourhoods where the crime rate is high. Their lack of financial resources prevents them from finding apartments that they can afford in safer neighbourhoods. Moving, then, offers no solution (Friedman 1976). Finally, certain aspects of their way of life increase their vulnerability to possible aggression. For instance, the fact that senior citizens are unable to defend themselves in case of attack is very evident; they have regular habits that can be easily noted and the date their pension cheques are delivered is generally public knowledge. This greatly increases the chances of a successful attack and heightens their general fear of crime.

The Canadian Urban Victimization Survey (Solicitor General of Canada 1983, 1984, 1985) shows that widows and widowers are more fearful than persons who still have their mates or who have never married. Furthermore, senior citizens living alone are generally more apt to fear for their personal safety (67% among women and 40% among men) than those who live with other adults (64% of women and 29% of men). Clemente and Kleiman (1976) report that 51% of persons 65 and over, in the United States, are afraid to go out alone at night against 41% of the rest of the sample. Sex makes an even greater difference: older women are afraid in 69% of the cases against 60% for the younger women; older men are afraid in 34% of cases against 19% for younger men.

The survey done by G.R.A.C. (Brillon *et al.* 1984) shows that age and sex make even more marked differences for the Canadian population. Among women, 60% of those 60 and over are fearful against 48% of younger women, while among the men, 17% of the oldest are fearful compared with 7% of the youngest. Not only the fact of being a woman leads to greater fear; elderly men express more fear than their younger counterparts. Socioeconomic status is another discriminant variable, with 51% of the poor senior citizens fearing attack against 43% of the more fortunate ones. Finally, the larger the community, the greater the people's fear, the elderly being proportionately more afraid than the young: 76% of the former living in large cities and 68% in the suburbs against 57% of the younger respondents living in large cities and 47% in the suburbs. Thus, old people living in cities of 50,000 or more inhabitants are more afraid of crime than other members of the population.

Victimization and Activities Outside the Home

The Canadian Urban Victimization Survey (Solicitor General of Canada 1983, 1984, 1985) concludes that one of the main reasons for the low rate of victimization among old people is that they expose themselves less to potentially dangerous situations, such as activities after dark. Whether because of age, illness or other factors associated with aging, or whether due to fear, the undeniable fact is that senior citizens, because of limited exposure, are victims of crime much less often than younger people. In the seven major cities of Canada (Solicitor General 1985: Bulletin No. 6), only 10% of persons 65 and over said they spent more than 20 evenings away from home each month as compared with about 45% of persons from 25 to 39 and 70% of persons under 25.

The fact of going out less often does not totally explain the low rate of victimization among elderly people. The nature of a person's activities is the essential key to the type and frequency of victimization. For example, according to the Canadian data, the rate of violent crimes for young people of 16 to 24 who go out from 10 to 20 times a month is 92 per 1000 inhabitants compared with 13 per 1000 inhabitants among persons 65 and over who go out just as often. This is because elderly people go less often to places such as bars, discotheques and nightclubs where the risks are potentially high. However, the same study shows that when senior citizens do go to these "dangerous" places, they stand as much chance as young people of being victims of personal theft and even more chance of being victims of robbery.

Type of Victimization and Fear of Crime

An American study (Shotland *et al.* 1979) shows that the fact of having been assaulted physically increases a person's fear and can possibly result in changes in behaviour. The study of the Solicitor General of Canada indicates that a direct and recent criminal attack heightens elderly people's fear, but no more nor less than other age groups. In other words, former victims would be more apt to be afraid than non-victims. Also, the findings of this Canadian survey seem to agree with those of Shotland *et al.* regarding the type of victimization in the case of elderly people. The study shows that among persons 65 and over, those who — in the past (before the year the survey was done) — had been attacked were much more fearful than the others: "Nine of every ten elderly women and five out of ten elderly men who had experienced an attack with loss of property feared for their personal safety. Those who had been attacked, but had not also suffered property loss were somewhat less likely to be fearful — 80% of women and 35% of men. Those who had experienced only property loss or damage were the least likely to be fearful — 70% of women and 30% of men" (Solicitor General 1985c: Bulletin No. 6, 3-4). The same thing was also true for women of 40 and over, as well as for men of 50 and over, but did not apply to younger people, that is, women under 40 and men under 50.

The research carried out by G.R.A.C. (Brillon *et al.* 1984) arrives at similar results. Of the total Canadian sample (N = 817), 161 respondents (20%) had already been victims of a crime against their person. Of these, the ones who avoided going out alone at night "often" or "very often" made up 24% of the victims under 60 and 58% of those 60 and over — evidence that age, associated with the type of victimization, has a real influence on the fear of crime. Furthermore, for the elderly, the fact of having previously been the victim of physical attack engenders much greater fear than it does in younger people. It shows that indirectly, fear of crime in elderly people is increased — on account of their failing strength — by dread of the psychological, material and above all, the physical consequences of a personal attack.

DIRECTIONS FOR RESEARCH ON CRIME AND THE ELDERLY

Criminological research, to date, has been largely limited to quantifying and describing victimization, fear of crime and the attitudes of the elderly toward the criminal justice system. Certain studies, particularly victimization surveys, have undertaken to compare various age groups to show the differences that exist between senior citizens and younger members of the population on the subject of crime and the behaviour it elicits, including prevention and protection measures. It is unfortunate that most of the research has no gerontological content — there is no specific reference to the effect of the aging process.

If, indeed, there is a direct link between age, victimization and the fear of crime, it has not yet been properly defined. It is certain that aging, for many people, means a slowing down of their activities, less coming and going and much more time spent at home. The fact of going about less often reduces, *ipso facto*, the degree of exposure to crime, hence the rate of victimization. It explains why senior citizens, in general, are victims of crime less often than other age groups. However, what we still do not know is to what extent the fear of crime is due to the aging process in restricting the activities of the elderly, and consequently reducing the probability of their becoming victims.

The research shows very little information in this regard. What future studies should be able to show is the relationship between aging and fear, between fear in general and fear of crime, between fear of crime and the lifestyle of the elderly. Obviously the fact of aging elicits fears because of greater personal vulnerability to accidents, illness, solitude and poverty. This vulnerability particularly affects women, because as a rule they live longer than men, and consequently there are many more among the 60 and over population. There are also proportionately more who live alone and who are financially in need.

The anxiety that aging evokes in some people is apt to be concretized as a fear of crime. It is hard to know, then, at exactly what point the fear of crime stems from a more general fear. According to the research, people who are more fearful than others by nature or temperament tend to develop a greater fear of crime, although the risk of their becoming a victim of criminal attack is not necessarily any greater.

Besides the study of the interdependency between fear of crime and dread of victimization, there should be research that concentrates more on an analysis of the way in which the fear elicited by crime influences the living conditions and thinking of elderly persons. This means taking into account the integration of senior citizens in their milieu, their family and social relationships, their living habits, their activities, their attitudes to society, their view of the world, and, of course, the principal elements that condition their way of life: income, health, psychological well-being, housing. Up to now, in criminological research, age was considered a subordinate variable that could explain certain attitudes to crime. The results obtained — as we have seen — give rise to more questions than they answer. That is why it is necessary, in our opinion, to change perspective and analyze attitudes to crime in terms of all the characteristics of the elderly. By taking this direction, the research would succeed in establishing more exactly the impact of aging on the anxiety creating process and more particularly, the impact of aging on the fear of crime and dread of victimization.

Living Conditions: Differences between Elderly Men and Elderly Women

Criminological studies make little reference to the fact that the living conditions of the elderly vary enormously according to sex. The differences are basic and have a direct impact on the fear of crime and victimization. The Montreal survey (Brillon 1986) shows, for example, that 72% of elderly men live with a mate compared with only 31% of the women. Others live with one of their children, or more rarely, with a friend. There are twice as many women (43%) as men (22%) who live alone. In addition to this solitude, there are financial problems. Twenty-eight percent of the men have annual incomes of less than $7,000, and 50% have incomes under $10,000. The situation is much worse for women. Half of them (51%) have to manage on less than $7,000 a year, and almost three quarters (71%) on less than $10,000.

Women's state of health also seems to be poorer than that of the men, 20% of them having had to take to their beds at least once during the year preceding the survey, as opposed to 8% of the men. Furthermore, although our sample comprised male and female populations of the same age distribution, 14% of the women had difficulty getting about alone against only 4% of the men. It is understood, then, that sex as a variable is counterbalanced in a way by income, solitude and difficulty in getting about alone. This may explain why 67% of the women "often" or "very often" avoid going out alone at night for fear of crime compared to 28% of the men. Physical vulnerability and poverty together create a difference in the degree of fear among elderly men and women, to the extent that the fact of avoiding going out at night "for fear of crime" is closely linked with sex[1], income[2] and solitude[3]; these three factors characterize the conditions of life for women of 60 and over much more than for men. Further studies should pay particular attention to the different way aging affects women and men.

Abuse of the Elderly

Today, more and more research is being focused on the maltreatment to which certain elderly people fall victim, either within their family or in nursing homes. These studies, however, are difficult and the value, significance and representative nature of the data they collect are often subject to serious reservations. The fact is that, in most cases, the study of elder abuse is done indirectly, based on the evidence of professionals (doctors, nurses, social workers, police, volunteer workers), who work in hospitals and nursing homes or with elderly people who live at home. These studies measure the frequency, nature and gravity of the abuse on the basis of what has come to the attention of these professionals, the descriptions they give and the cases they report.

It is difficult to measure the extent of the violence perpetrated against senior citizens by this method. Most of these studies are too imprecise to be able to evaluate the percentage of old people who are victims of abuse in proportion to the number of senior citizens in the care of professionals, and even less in proportion to all persons of 60, 65 and over. This difficulty in quantifying the number of elderly victims of abuse is a problem that is pratically insurmountable at the moment. There are two reasons for this. Firstly the abusive behaviour is not overt and therefore not "visible". Secondly, victims who live with relatives or in nursing homes are "dependent" on their aggressors and are afraid to denounce them for fear of reprisals. Since it is hardly possible to force one's way into private homes, a great deal of violence goes on unobserved. What is to be done?

As far as research is concerned, it is conceivable — at least with senior citizens who are still relatively autonomous — to undertake surveys by means of personal interviews, and to learn first-hand of any experience of family violence. In the United States, Strauss *et al.* (1980) showed that it was possible by this methodological approach to get information from both the victims and the perpetrators of the abuse. As for Steinmetz (1983), she focused her research on elder abuse on American volunteers who admitted they had used force against their parents. This method offers a direct approach to family violence and enables the researcher to analyze it in such a way as to show the interaction that exists between aggressor and victim.

We share the opinion of Yin (1985) concerning the orientation of future research:

> It appears that surveys of the elderly population, even local ones, are needed to provide reliable estimates of the extent of elder abuse in the community. Continual reliance on the opinions of clinical professionals or detected cases of elder abuse as data would not improve current knowledge of the prevalence of elder abuse (p. 115).

The above type of survey is obviously less applicable in nursing homes or in the geriatric wards of hospitals. Since the average age in these institutions is about 80, and since many of these patients suffer from loss of memory and mental confusion, it would be better to proceed, as Stannard (1973) did, with a participant observation study in order to discover under what institutional and social conditions the abuses occur in such settings.

In Canada, there are so few studies on the abuse of the elderly that all research is of considerable importance. It is essential that both federal and provincial governments, not only encourage, but foster research on the social and criminal violence perpetrated against the elderly. It is also necessary that public policies be developed to protect our senior citizens, ensure their security and a decent quality of life, as well as procure for them a minimum of well-being and recognition on the part of the entire community.

SOCIAL POLICIES FOR THE ELDERLY

Unfortunately, Canada does not yet have social policies specifically designed to give senior citizens material and psychological security. At the moment, the programs that exist, for the most part, are the result of individual or community initiatives, and vary enormously from one region to another. It is up to the government to adopt policies that answer the most urgent needs of senior citizens and implement programs that will give them a sense of security.

First of all, it seems imperative to us that the primary object of any social policy for senior citizens should be to keep them in their homes. This means measures to help elderly men and women who live alone as well as to assist persons, relatives or friends, who have senior citizens in their care.

One of the first things to be done is for the legislator to adopt a law on the "protection of the elderly" that will fight both institutional and domestic abuse. The function of this law would be to define abuse, make denunciation easier and encourage the senior citizens themselves to stand up for their rights. In the United States, where several States passed special legislation in 1974 to protect the aged, the number of cases of abuse reported by the public in general and by other sources, such as the police, service agencies, courts, hospitals and visiting nurses, increased appreciably. Such legislative measures should be accompanied by the creation of an Ombudsman whose jurisdiction would extend to nursing homes and all public services dispensed to senior citizens, whether in institutions or at home. Thus, victims would know who to go to when wronged within programs directly or indirectly dependent on government organizations. Still at the general level, it is important that a parliamentary commission of enquiry be created to take stock of the situation regarding "violence and the elderly". This commission could suggest programs to the government that would improve the fate of old people, prevent the abuses and crimes to which they are subjected and enhance their safety and their sense of security.

More specifically, as Lawton (1980–1981) suggests, programs should be implemented at the national, provincial and municipal levels, (a) to inform the elderly of the dangers that threaten them; (b) to lessen their vulnerability and their fear; (c) to come to the aid of the victims of criminal acts or abuse and (d) to prevent any kind of victimization.

Informing the Elderly of the Dangers that Threaten Them

On the question of informing senior citizens of the potential danger of victimization, every time the subject is brought up, some people claim that doing so only increases their fear, already irrational and exaggerated. This attitude is understandable, although not very logical. It is tantamount to not warning children to beware of strangers who offer them candy or a ride in their car. It is like avoiding the subject of rape for fear of causing young girls undue anxiety. These examples show that preventive information is necessary if we want to avoid serious incidents that may occur if we do not want to talk about them because they are so serious that they would necessarily arouse people's fear. There is no use ignoring the situation. The saying "Forewarned is forearmed" applies here. In other words, to be prepared, one has to know the possible danger. The problem is not the information itself, but the way it is conveyed. Senior citizens must be advised to be vigilant, to be careful not to expose themselves to danger and not to leave themselves open to victimization.

For these reasons, efforts should be made to warn senior citizens about the crimes to which they could fall victim and tell them how to protect themselves against these crimes. The police, or other practitioners, should give regular talks at golden age clubs or associations for retirees on the following topics: How to protect one's home against burglary; how to avoid fraud; how to avoid and deal with street crime. By means of such talks, using audiovisual material, senior citizens could be shown simple measures for protecting their home, precautions to take during prolonged absences and how to protect themselves when going about in the city. By educating older people in prevention, it is possible, at little expense, to reduce the incidence of certain crimes.

The police should give these educational initiatives logistic support. In a number of American cities the police visit the lodgings of senior citizens, inspect them for weak points and suggest ways in which they can be effectively protected against burglary. Volunteer retirees could contribute their services to seniors unable to install protective hardware and have their valuables engraved by doing these things for them or for people who do not have the financial means to pay to have them done.

Reducing the Vulnerability of the Elderly

Many senior citizens are vulnerable because they are physically handicapped or because, in the eyes of potential criminals, they look like easy prey. To lessen this vulnerability, measures should be taken to increase the actual competence of the older person (*i.e.*, better glasses, a hearing aid) or perceived competence (*i.e.*, peer support group). This should increase the self-confidence of elderly people and make them more aware of the potential threat of victimization. Moreover, senior citizens should be warned not to keep too many valuables or a great deal of money at home or on their person. Carrying a considerable amount of money inevitably exposes a person, not necessarily to attack, but certainly to a greater loss, should one occur.

To prevent certain thefts, the government services should deposit welfare cheques or old age pensions directly in the beneficiary's bank account, rather than send them by mail. Since these are the principal sources of income for persons of 65 and over in 75% of cases, a measure of this kind would considerably lessen their vulnerability to theft. For some seniors, going to the bank is a frightening experience. Because the date pension cheques arrive is general knowledge, their theft is fairly frequent, with often disastrous consquences for the victim.

Transportation and shopping escorts are additional ways to protect and ensure the safety of older people. Such services should be developed and made generally available to all senior citizens who would like to take advantage of them. Another way to lessen the vulnerability of the elderly is to break through their solitude, and see that they are not isolated. A telephone check-in program is very reassuring to older people, especially those who live alone, and it is also a means of knowing whether anything has happened to them.

Helping Victims of Abuse and Crime

In Canada, federal and provincial laws guarantee certain compensation to all victims of violent crime. In the case of senior citizens who have a low income, the government should compensate for any material losses that affect the person's living conditions and involve the deprivation of essential needs, such as food, medicine and heating.

There should also be a network of receiving centres for elderly victims to afford them a place of refuge when they are being ill-treated and a change of milieu has proved necessary or when, after having been abused, they can no longer stay alone because the experience has traumatized them. Counseling services should be available in these cases. Similarly, for victims who have to go to the police or to the courts, a support person, such as a lawyer or a social worker, should be provided to help with the process of pressing charges or acting as a witness.

Acting Collectively to Prevent Rather than Cure

An effort should be made in neighbourhoods and communities to integrate senior citizens in crime prevention programs. As we have seen, feeling incapable of doing anything to counter crime and a sense of alienation largely explain elderly people's great fear of crime. There is, therefore, a need to involve them in community projects such as voluntary patrols, block watch and defensible space programs.

It is important that seniors be made aware of the considerable role they can play in the surveillance of their neighbourhood. Since they are often at home, they can become additional "eyes and ears" for the police. In the United States, "seniors are often given identification cards, window stickers and even portable radios to enhance their willingness to protect themselves and become ubiquitous witnesses" (Corrigan 1981). To involve them in this way in community preventive action is an effective way of making them feel useful as well as allaying their fear, which is often out of proportion to the real risk of their being victimized.

CONCLUSION

The data we have analyzed in this monograph clearly show that in elderly people there is an interaction between both the "material conditions of life" (income, neighbourhood, type of residence etc.) and the "style of life" (degree of exposure, types of activity, places frequented etc.) on the one hand, and criminal and social victimization (whether subjective or objective) on the other. It turns out, too, that these two variables (conditions and style of life) have an influence on fear in general as well as fear of crime in particular. It also seems that the feeling of vulnerability (which increases with age) possibly underlies these interactions between "way of life", "victimization", "general fear" and "fear of crime".

It must be remembered that among the elderly, realities such as fear, victimization and vulnerability are experienced at two different levels: one that is general and subjective (fear of crime; feeling of vulnerability and fear of life in general), the other concrete and objective (actual experience of criminal victimization; real fear motivated by crime; physical or psychic vulnerability due to handicaps or illness). All these elements emanate, at least in part, from the conditions and style of life, and they also interact one with the other. The model is complex, and for this reason, future research should make a distinction between fear of crime and a general feeling of fear, real vulnerability and a feeling of being vulnerable, criminal victimization and social victimization, and the actual experience of being victimized and fear of being victimized.

To arrive at a better understanding of the attitudes of older people to violence, it is essential to know the characteristics unique to their way of life, their thinking, degree of social integration, their view of the world, their concerns and expectations. Consequently, to effectively deal with the fear of crime and a sense of insecurity felt by elderly people, a combined criminological and gerontological approach is essential.

NOTES

1. Pearson's correlation is $r = .39$ ($p = .001$)
2. Pearson's correlation is $r = .17$ ($p = .006$)
3. Pearson's correlation is $r = .19$ ($p = .003$)

BIBLIOGRAPHY

Adams, R., and T. Smith
    1976   *Fear of Neighbourhood*, National Opinion Research Center Report 127C on the Social Change Project, National Research Center, Chicago.

Anderson, C. L.
    1981   "Abuse and Neglect Among the Elderly." *Journal of Gerontological Nursing* 7 (2): 77-85.

Antunes, G., F. L. Cook, T. D. Cook, and W. G. Skogan
    1977   "Patterns of Personal Crime Against the Elderly: Findings from a National Survey." *The Gerontologist* 17: 320-329.

Ashton, N.
    1981   "Senior Citizens' Views of Crime and the Criminal Justice System." In O. Lister (ed.) *The Elderly Victim of Crime*, Springfield, Illinois: Charles C. Thomas, Publisher.

Baril, M.
    1984   L'envers du crime. Etude victimologique. Centre International de Criminologie Comparée, Université de Montréal, Les Cahiers de Recherches Criminologiques no 2.

Bélanger, L, Th. Darche, H. de Ravinel, et P. Grenier
    1981   "Violence et personnes âgées." Rapport du Comité Violence et Personnes Agées. *Les Cahiers de l'Association Québécoise de Gérontologie* 1, mars 1981.

Bellot, S., et D. Elie
    1983   Le vol à main armée au Québec. Rapport final no 1. Description statistique. Centre international de criminologie comparée. Université de Montréal.

Bertrand, M.-A.
    1980   "Quelques apports de la criminologie et de la victimologie à la compréhension du phénomène de la violence à l'endroit des personnes âgées. Conférence prononcée devant l'Association Québécoise de Gérontologie." Colloque sur la violence et les personnes âgées. In L. Bélanger *et al.* (1981) *Les Cahiers de l'Association Québécoise de Gérontologie* 1 (mars).

Biderman, A. D., A. Johnson, J. McIntyre, and A. W. Weir
    1967   *Report on a Pilot Study in the District of Columbia on Victimization and Attitudes Toward Law Enforcement.* Field Surveys 1, conducted for the President's Commission on Law Enforcement and Administration of Justice. Washington, D.C.: Government Printing Office.

Block, M., and J. P. Sinnott (eds.)
   1979   *The Battered Elder Syndrome: An Exploratory Study*. College Park, Md.: University of Maryland, Center On Aging.
Block, R.
   1979   "Community, Environment and Violent Crime." *Criminology* 17: 46–57.
Boggs, S. S.
   1971   "Formal and Informal Crime Control: An exploratory Study on Urban, Suburban, and Rural Orientations." *Sociological Quarterly* 12: 1–9.
Braungart, M., W. Hoyer, and R. Braungart
   1979   "Fear of Crime and the Elderly." In A. Goldstein, W. Hoyer, and P. Monti (eds.), *Police and the Elderly*. New York: Pergamon.
Braungart, M., R. Braungart, and W. Hoyer
   1980   "Age, Sex and Social Factors in Fear of Crime." *Sociological Focus* 13 (1) 55–56.
Brillon, Y.
   1983   "La peur du crime et la punitivité chez les personnes âgées." *Criminologie* XVI: 7–30.
   1984a   "Les attitudes des Canadiens vis-à-vis de la police." *Canadian Journal of Criminology* 26 (2/April): 133–147.
   1984b   "Les attitudes punitives dans la population canadienne." *Canadian Journal of Criminology* 26 (3/July): 293–313.
   1985a   "La confiance des Canadiens dans la justice pénale." *Canadian Journal of Criminology* 26 (3/July): 271–289.
   1985b   "Public Opinion About the Penal System: A Cynical View of Criminal Justice." In Gibson and Baldwin (eds.) *Law in a Cynical Society?* Calgary-Vancouver: Carswell Legal Publications, Western Division.
   1986   "Les personnes âgées face au crime." Centre International de Criminologie Comparée. Montréal: Université de Montréal. Rapport de Recherche.
Brillon, Y., M.-M. Cousineau, and S. Gravel
   1983   Rapport préliminaire sur un sondage auprès des personnes âgées de Montréal. Manuscrit non publié. C.I.C.C. Université de Montréal.
Brillon, Y., Ch. Louis-Guerin, et M. Ch. Lamarche
   1984   *Attitudes of the Canadian Public Toward Crime Policies*. Group Research on Attitudes toward Crime, G.R.A.C., University of Montreal.
Brock, A.
   1980   "Editorial: Stop abuse of the elderly." *Journal of Gerontological Nursing* 6 (4): 191.
Brown, D.
   1976   "Canada and the Noose." An Interview with H. Mohr. *Quest* (May/June).
Brown, L.P. and M. A. Young Rifai
   1976   "Crime Prevention for Older Americans: Multnomah County's Victimization Study." *Police Chief* 43 (February): 38–42.
Bureau of Regional Operations of the Pennsylvania Commission on Crime and Delinquency
   1984   "Strategies to Reduce the Incidence and Impact of Crime that Victimizes the Elderly in Pennsylvania." In Joseph J. Costa (ed.): *Abuse of the*

Elderly: A Guide to Resources and Services. Lexington, Massachusetts: Lexington Books, Heath.

Burkhardt, J., and L. Newton
1979   "Crime and the Elderly: Their Perception and Their Reaction, Montgomery Police Department, abstracted in U.S. Department of Justice." In G. Boston, R. Nitzberg, M. Kravitz (eds.), *Criminal Justice and the Elderly*, Law Enforcement Assistance Agency; National Criminal Justice Reference Service.

Butler, R.
1975   *Why Survive? Being Old in America*. New York: Harper and Row.

Canadian Governmental Report on Aging
1982   Ministère des Approvisionnements et Services. Ottawa: no de cat. H 21/1982 A.

Cantor, M. H.
1980   "The Informal Support System: Its Relevance in the Lives of the Elderly." In E. Borgotta and N. G. McClusky (eds.), *Aging and Society: Current Research and Policy Perspectives*. Beverly Hills: Sage Publications.

Chappell, N. L., L. A. Strain and A. A. Blandford
1986   *Aging and Health Care: A Social Perspective*. Toronto: Holt, Rinehart and Winston of Canada, Limited.

Chen, Pei N., Sharon L. Bell, Debra L. Dolinsky, John Doyle and Moira Dunn
1981   "Elderly abuse in domestic settings: A pilot study." *Journal of Gerontological Social Work* 4 (1): 3–17.

Christie, N.
1974   Definition of Violent Behaviour. XXIII International Course in Criminology. Maracaibo, Venezuela: July 28th to August 3rd.

Clarke, R., P. Ekblom, M. Hough and P. Mayhew
1985   "Elderly Victims of Crime and Exposure to Risk." *The Howard Journal* 24 (1/February): 1–10.

Clarke, A. H. and M. J. Lewis
1982   "Fear of Crime Among the Elderly," *British Journal of Criminology* 22 (1): 49–62.

Clemente, F. and M. Kleiman
1976   "Fear of Crime Among the Aged," *The Gerontologist*, 16 (3) 207–210.

Cohn, E., L. Kidder and J. Harvey
1979   "Crime Prevention vs. Victimization Prevention: The Psychology of Two Different Reactions." *Victimology* 3 (3/4): 285–296.

Conklin, J. E.
1975   *The Impact of Crime*. New York: Macmillan Publishing Co. Inc.
1976   "Robbery, the Elderly, and Fear: An urban problem in search of solution." Pp. 99–110 in J. Goldsmith and S. S. Goldsmith (eds.), *Crime and the Elderly: Challenge and Response*. Lexington, Mass.: Lexington Books, Heath.
1981   *Criminology*, New York: Macmillian Publishing Co., Inc.

Cook, F. L.
1976   "Criminal Victimization of the Elderly: A New National Problem?" In E. C. Viano, *Victims and Society*. Washington: Visage Press.
1980   "Testing Claims about Criminal Victimization of the Elderly: Toward

Age Based or Age Irrelevant Policies." Paper presented at the American Society of Criminology, San Francisco (Calif.) November 5.

Cook, F. L., and T. D. Cook
1976   "Evaluating the Rhetoric of Crisis: A Case Study of Criminal Victimization of the Elderly." *Social Service Review* 50(4): 633–646.

Cook, F.L., W. G. Skogan, T. D. Cook, and G. E. Antunes
1978   "Criminal Victimization of the Elderly: The Physical and Economic Consequences." *The Gerontologist* 18 (4/August): 338–350.

Corrado, R. R., R. Roesch, W. Glakman, J. L. Evans, and G. J. Leger
1980   "Life Styles and Personal Victimization: a test of the model with the Canadian survey data." *Journal of Crime and Justice* 3: 129–301.

Corrigan, R. S.
1981   "Crime Prevention Programs for the Elderly." In Lester, D. (ed.), *The Elderly Victim of Crime*. Springfield, Illinois: Charles C. Thomas.

Costa, J. J.
1984   *Abuse of the Elderly. A Guide to Resource and Services*. Lexington, Mass.: Lexington Books, Heath.

Cousineau, M.-M.
1987   Perception, Réaction et Attitudes Des Personnes Âgées À L'Égard Du Crime De La Justice. Thèse de maîtrise. Ecole de Criminologie, Université de Montréal.

C.R.O.P. Inc.
1980   "Sondage omnibus." Omnibus 1980-5-3. Montréal.

Creighton, Judy
1986   "Selon deux sociologues torontois: les vieillards en institution traités comme des enfants." Montréal: La Presse, March 19, 1986: k. 7.

Cunningham, C. L.
1975   *The Pattern of Crime Against the Aging: The Kansas City Study*. Speech to the National Conference on Crime Against the Elderly. Washington, June 5.
1976   *Pattern and Effect of Crime Against the Aging: The Kansas City Study*. In Jack Goldsmith and Sharon Goldsmith, *Crime and the Elderly*. Lexington, Mass.: Lexington Books, Heath.

Cusson, M.
1986   "L'analyse stratégique et quelques développements récents en criminologie." *Criminologie* XIX (1): 53–73.

van Dijk, J. J. M., and C. Steinmetz
1983   "Victimization Surveys: beyond measuring the volume of crime." *Victimology* 8: 291–301.

Doob, A. N. and J. Roberts
1982   Crime: Some Views of the Canadian Public. Toronto: Centre of Criminology.
1983   *An Analysis of the Public's View of Sentencing*. Ottawa: Department of Justice. Canada.

Douglass, R. L., and T. Hickey
1983   Domestic Neglect and Abuse of the Elderly: Research findings and a systems perspective for service delivery planning. Pp. 115–134 in J. I. Kosberg (ed.), *Abuse and Maltreatment of the Elderly: Causes and interventions*. Boston, Bristol, London: John Wright, PSG Inc.

Dubow, F., E. McCabe, and G. Kaplan
  1979   *Reaction to Crime, A Critical Review of the Literature*. U.S. Department of Justice. Law Enforcement Assistance Administration. National Institute of Law Enforcement and Criminal Justice.

Dussick, J. P., and C. J. Eichman
  1976   "The Elderly Victim." In Goldsmith and S. S. Goldsmith (eds.), *Crime and the Elderly*. Lexington, Mass.: Lexington Books, Heath.

Eastman, M., and M. Sutton
  1982   "Granny Battering." *Geriatric Medicine*, November: 11–15.

Elmore, E.
  1981   "Consumer Fraud and the Elderly." In Lester, D. (ed.): *The Elderly Victim of Crime*, Springfield, Illinois: Charles C. Thomas, Publisher.

Erskine, H.
  1974   "The Polls: Fear of Violence and Crime." *Public Opinion Quarterly* Spring (38): 131–145.

Felson, M. and L. E. Cohen
  1980   "Human Ecology and Crime: A Routine Activity Approach." *Human Ecology* 8: 384–406.

Figgie, H. E.
  1980   *The Figgie Report on Fear of Crime: America Afraid: Part 1: The General Public*. Ohio: A-T-O Inc.

Fowler, F. J., and T. W. Mangione
  1974   "The Nature of Fear." Survey Research Program, University of Massachusetts and the joint Center for Urban Studies of MIT, Harvard University (September). Paper.

Fréchette, P.
  1984   "Le vol avec effraction: profil de son auteur." *Sûreté* Nov.: 11–22.

Friedman, D. M.
  1976   "A Service Model for Elderly Crime Victims." In Goldsmith, J. and S. S. Goldsmith (eds.). *Crime and the Elderly*. Lexington, Mass. D.C. Heath and Company.

Furstenberg, F. F., Jr.
  1971   "Public Reaction to Crime in the Streets." *American Scholar*, 40 (4): 601–610.
  1972   "Fear of Crime and its Effects on Citizen Behavior." In A. Biderman (ed.), *Crime and Justice: A Symposium*. New York: Nailburg.

Garofalo, J.
  1979   "Victimization and Fear of Crime." *Journal of Research in Crime and Delinquency* January (16): 80–97.

Geis, G.
  1976   "Defrauding the Elderly." In J. Goldsmith and S. S. Goldsmith (eds.), *Crime and the Elderly*, Lexington, Mass.: Lexington Books, Heath.
  1977   "The Terrible Indignity: Crimes against the Elderly." In M. S. Young Rifai: *Justice and Older Americans*. Lexington, Mass.: Lexington Books, Heath.

Gil, D. G.
  1970   *Violence Against Children: Physical Abuse in the United States*. Cambridge, Mass.: Harvard University Press.

Golant, S. M.
   1972   "The Residential Location and Spatial Behavior of the Elderly: A Cana-
           dian Example." Research paper no 143, Department of Geography. Uni-
           versity of Chicago.
Goldsmith, J.
   1976   "Police and the Older Victim." *Police Chief* 43: 24–27.
Goldsmith, J., and S. S. Goldsmith (eds.)
   1976   *Crime and the Elderly*. Lexington, Mass.: Lexington Books, Heath.
Goldsmith, J., and N. E. Tomas
   1974   "Crime Against the Elderly: A Continuing National Crisis." *Aging*. June
           236: 10–13.
Goldstein, A. P., W. J. Hoyer, and P. J. Monty (eds.)
   1979   *Police and the Elderly*. New York: Pergamon Press.
G.R.A.C. (Group for Research on Attitudes Toward Crime)
   1984   Brillon, Y.; Ch. Louis-Guerin and M.-Ch. Lamarche: *The Attitudes of
           the Canadians toward Crime Policies*, Report no 1A, Criminological
           Research Collection: Montreal, C.I.C.C., Université de Montréal.
Groupe de Recherche sur les Attitudes Envers la Criminalité
   1982   Les attitudes du public canadien envers les politiques criminelles. Les
           Cahiers de Recherches Criminologiques, Cahier no 1. Centre Interna-
           tional de Criminologie Comparée, G.R.A.C., Université de Montréal.
Grossman, D. A.
   1977   *Reducing the Impact of Crime Against the Elderly: A Survey and
           Appraisal of Existing and Potential Programs*. Hollywood, California:
           Media Five.
Gubrium, J. F.
   1984   "Victimization in Old Age: Available Evidence and Three Hypotheses."
           In Joseph J. Costa (ed.), *Abuse of the Elderly: A Guide to Resources and
           Services*. Lexington, Mass.: Lexington Books, Heath.
Hacker, G. A.
   1977   "Nursing Homes: Social Victimization of the Elderly," Pp. 63–71 in
           M. A. Young Rifai (ed.), *Justice and Older Americans*. Lexington,
           Mass.: Lexington Books.
Hahn, P. H.
   1976   *Crime Against the Elderly: A Study of Victimology*. Santa Cruz: Davis
           Publication.
Harris, C. (ed.)
   1978   *Fact Book on Aging: A Profile of America's Older Population*. Wash-
           ington, D.C.: National Council on the Aging.
Harris, L.
   1975   *The myth and reality of aging in America*. Washington, D.C.: National
           Council on Aging.
Hartnagel, T.
   1979   "The Perception and Fear of Crime: Implications for Neighborhood,
           Social Activity, and Community Affect." *Social Forces* 58 (1): 176–193.
Hickey, T. and R. L. Douglass
   1981a   "Neglect and Abuse of Older Family Members: Professionals' Perspec-
           tives and Case Experiences." *The Gerontologist* 21 (2): 171–177.

1981b "Mistreatment of the Elderly in the Domestic Setting: An exploratory Study." *American Journal of Public Health*, 71 (5/May): 500–507.

Hindelang, M. J.
1976 *Criminal Victimization in Eight American Cities*. Cambridge, Mass.: Ballinger.

Hindelang, M. J., C. S. Duss, P. T. Sutton, and A. L. Aumick
1977 *Source Book of Criminal Justice Statistics*, 1976. Washington, D.C., U.S. Dept. of Justice L.E.A.A., U.S. Government Printing Office.

Hindelang, M. J., M. R. Gottfredson, and J. Garofalo
1978 *Victims of Personal Crime: An Empirical Foundation for a Theory of Personal Victimization*. Cambridge, Mass.: Ballinger.

Hirschel, J. D., and K. B. Rubin
1982 "Special Problem Faced by the Elderly Victims of Crime." *Journal of Sociology and Social Welfare* 9 (2/June): 357–374.

Hochstedler, E.
1981 *Crime against the Elderly in 26 cities*, Criminal Justice Research Center. Albany, New York: U.S. Department of Justice.

Hough, J. M., R. V. G. Clarke, and P. Mayhew
1980 "Introduction." In R. V. G. Clarke and P. Mayhew's *Designing out Crime*. London: Her Majesty's Stationary Office.

Hough, M. and P. Mayhew
1983 The British Crime Survey: First Report (Home Office Research Study No. 76). London: H.M.S.O.

Hoyer, W. J.
1979 "The Elderly: Who Are They?" In A. P. Goldstein, W. J. Hoyer, and P. J. Monti (eds.), *Police and the Elderly*. New York: Pergamon Press.

Janson, P., and L. K. Ryder
1983 "Crime and the Elderly: The Relationship Between Risk and Fear." *The Gerontologist* 23, (2/April): 207–212.

Jaycox, V. H.
1978 "The Elderly's Fear of Crime: Rational or Irrational?" *Victimology: An International Journal* 3: 329–334.

Jayewardene, T. J., T. J. Juliani, and C. K. Talbot
1983 The Elderly as Victims of Crime. Crime Victims. Working Paper No. 5. Research and Statistics Section. Policy Planning and Development Branch. Department of Justice. Canada.

Kahana, E., J. Liang, B. Felton, T. Fairchild, and Z. Harel
1977 "Perspective of Aged on Victimization, Ageism, and Their Problems in Urban Society." *The Gerontologist* 17 (2): 121–129.

Kashmeri, Zuhair
1986 "100,000 elderly Canadians abused a year, panel says." *The Globe and Mail*, Toronto (March 28, 1986): A11.

Katz, K.
1979–
80 "Elder Abuse." *Journal of Family Law* 18 (4): 695–722.

Katzenbach, N. de B. *et al.*
1967 *The Challenge of Crime in a Free Society*. Washington: U.S. Government Printing Office.

Kegels, M. L.
1982   "Actualité bibliographique: Le crime, puisqu'il faut l'appeler par son nom ...: La peur du crime", *Déviance et Société* VI (2/trim/juin) 209–221.

Kennedy, L. W. and H. Krahn
1983   "Rural-Urban Origins and Fear of Crime: The Case for 'Rural Baggage'." Edmonton Area Series, Report No. 28. Department of Sociology. The University of Alberta. Edmonton, Alberta.

Kennedy, L. W., and R. A. Silverman
1985   "Significant Others and Fear of Crime among the Elderly." In *Int'l J. On Aging and Human Development* 20 (4) 1984–85.

King, N. R.
1984   "Exploitation and Abuse of Older Family Members: An Overview of the Problem." In Joseph J. Costa (ed.), *Abuse of the Elderly: A Guide to Resources and Services*. Lexington, Mass.: Lexington Books, Heath.

Kleinman, P., and D. David
1973   "Victimization and Perception of Crime in a Ghetto Community." *Criminology* 11:3 307–343.

Kosberg, J. (ed.)
1983   *Abuse and Maltreatment of the Elderly: Causes and Interventions*. Boston, Bristol, London: John Wright-PSG Inc.

Kosberg, J. I.
1983   "The Special Vulnerability of Elderly Parents." Pp. 263–277 in J. I. Kosberg (ed.), *Abuse and Maltreatment of the Elderly: Causes and Interventions*. Boston, Bristol, London: John Wright—PSG Inc.

Lagrange, H.
1983   Perception de la violence et sentiment d'insécurité. Enquête sur un échantillon représentatif de la population grenobloise. Série Analyses et Commentaires, No. 3, Banque de données socio-politiques: Grenoble. France.

Lamarche, M.-Ch. et Y. Brillon
1983   Les personnes âgées de Montréal face au crime. Une recherche qualitative. Groupe de recherche sur les attitudes envers la criminalité (G.R.A.C.). Montréal: Université de Montréal, C.I.C.C.

Lamont, C.
1985   La violence à domicile faite aux femmes âgées. Travail présenté pour le Cour EAN 6670: "Condition féminine et éducation continue." Université de Montréal.

Lau, E. E. and Kosberg. J. I.
1979   "Abuse of the Elderly by Informal Care Providers." *Aging*, No. 229-300, (September/October): 10/16.

Laurier, M.
1982   "Prévention en santé mentale: la qualité de vie des citoyens âgés repose sur la volonté politique de l'Etat." *Le Devoir* 73 (154): 2.

Lawton, M. P.
1980–81 "Crime Victimization and the Fortitude of the Aged." *Aged Care and Services Review* 2 (4): 20–31.

Lawton, M. P., L. Mahemow, S. Yaffe, and S. Feldman
  1976 "Psychological Aspects of Crime and Fear of Crime," in J. Goldsmith and S. S. Goldsmith (eds.), *Crime and the Elderly*. Lexington, Mass.: Lexington Books, Heath.

Lawton, M. P., and S. Yaffe
  1980 Victimization and Fear of Crime in Elderly Public Housing Tenants. Pp. 768–779 in *Journal of Gerontology* 35 (5).

Lebowitz, B.
  1975 "Age and Fearfulness: Personal and Situational Factors." *Journal of Gerontology*. 30 (6): 696–700.

Lecours, W., and J. Roy
  1982 "Violence and the Marginalization of the Elderly in Today's Society." *Canada's Mental Health* (September 1982): 25–28.

Lee, G. R.
  1982a "Sex Differences in Fear of Crime Among Older People," *Research on Aging*, 4 (3): 284–298.
  1982b "Residential Location and Fear of Crime Among the Elderly." *Rural Sociology* 47 (4): 655–669.
  1983 "Social Integration and Fear of Crime Among Older Persons." *Journal of Gerontology* 38 (6): 745–750.

Legal Research and Services for the Elderly of Massachusetts
  1984 "Elder Abuse in Massachusetts: A Survey of Professionals and Paraprofessionals." In Joseph J. Costa (ed.), *Abuse of the Elderly: A Guide to Resources and Services*. Lexington, Mass.: Lexington Books, Heath.

Lester, D.
  1981 *The Elderly Victim of Crime*. Springfield, Illinois: Charles C. Thomas Publisher.

Levitan, S.
  1976 *Programs in Aid of the Poor*. Baltimore: Johns Hopkins University Press.

Liang, J., and M. C. Sengstock
  1981 "The Risk of Personal Victimization Among the Aged." *Journal of Gerontology* 36: 463–71.

Lindquist, J. A., and J. M. Duke
  1982 "The Elderly Victim at Risk." *Criminology* 20 (1/May): 115–127.

Loether, H. J.
  1975 "Problems of Aging." *Sociological and Social Psychological Perspectives* (2e ed.). Cal.: Dickenson Publishing Company Inc.

Logan, M. M.
  1979 "Crime Against the Elderly: Cruel and Unusual Punishment." *Victimology* 4 (1): 129–132.

Lomax, F. *et al.*
  1978 "Criminal Victimization of the Elderly: The Physical and Economic Consequences." *Gerontologist* 18: 338–349.

Louis-Guerin, Ch.
   1983   La peur du crime: mythes et réalités. *Criminologie* XVI, (1): 69–83.
Main, B.
   1978   *Whole Person After Sixty: Crime and the Elderly.* Lexington, Mass.: Lexington Books, Heath.
Malinchak, A.
   1980   *Crime and Gerontology.* New Jersey: Prentice-Hall, Englewood Cliffs.
Malinchak, A., and D. Wright
   1978   "Older Americans and Crime: The Scope of Elderly Victimization." *Aging* (March/April): 10–16.
Markson, E. and B. Hess
   1980   "Older Women in the City." *Signs* 5 (3): 127–141.
Masse, J. C., et M. M. T. Brault
   1984   "Présentations: Sociétés, vieillissement et stratification des âgés." *Sociologie et Sociétés* XVI (2/October): 3–15.
Mawby, R. I.
   1982   "Crime and the Elderly: a review of British and American research." *Current Psychological Reviews* 2: 301–310.
McDaniel, S. A.
   1986   *Canada's Aging Population.* Toronto and Vancouver: Butterworths.
McMurray, H. L.
   1983   The Criminal Victimization of the Elderly. Occasional Paper No. 22. Institute of Urban Affairs and Research. Howard University: Washington, D.C.
McPherson, B. D.
   1983   *Aging as a Social Process.* An Introduction to Individual and Population Aging. Toronto: Butterworths.
National Council of Welfare
   1984   *Sixty-Five and Older.* Ottawa, Ontario: Minister of Supply and Services.
Norton, L. and M. Courlander
   1982   "Fear of Crime among the Elderly: The Role of Crime Prevention Programs." *The Gerontologist* 22 (4): 388–393.
O'Malley, H. et al.
   1979   *Elderly Abuse in Massachusetts: A Survey of Professionnals and Paraprofessionals.* Boston: Legal Research and Services for the Elderly.
O'Malley, T. A., H. C. O'Malley, D. E. Everitt, and D. Sarson
   1984   "Categories of Family-mediated Abuse and Neglect of Elderly Persons." *Journal of the American Geriatrics Society* Vol. 32 (5/May): 362–370.
O'Rourke, M.
   1981   "Elder Abuse: The State of the Art." Paper prepared for the National Conference on the Abuse of Older Persons, Boston, Mass. March 23–25.
Patterson, A.
   1979   Training the Elderly in Mastery of the Environment. In A. P. Goldstein, W. J. Hoyer, and P. J. Monti (eds.), *Police and the Elderly.* New York: Pergamon.
Peyrefitte, A.
   1981   *Les chevaux du lac Ladoga.* Paris: Plon.

Pfuhl, J. J.
    1980   Fear of Crime: A Test of the Community Integration Hypothesis. Presented at the Annual Meeting of the American Criminological Society. San Francisco.

Pollack, L., and A. H. Patterson
    1980   "Territoriality and Fear of Crime in Elderly and Nonelderly Homeowners." *Journal of Social Psychology* III: 119–129.

Pope, C. E.
    1976   "A Review of Recent Trends: The Effects of Crime on the Elderly." *Police Chief* (February): 48–51.

Pope, C. E., and W. Feyerheim
    1976   "The Effects of Crime on the Elderly: A Review of Recent Trends." *Police Chief* 43: 29–32.

Powell, D. E.
    1980   "The Crimes Against the Elderly." *Journal of Gerontological Work* 3 (1/fall): 27–39.

President's Commission on Law Enforcement and Administration of Justice
    1967   *The Challenge of Crime in a Free Society*. Washington, D.C.: Government Printing Office.

Radio Canada, CBFT
    1986   Emission de télévision. "Le Point." Montréal: February 27, 1986.

Ragan, P. K.
    1977   "Crimes Against the Elderly: Findings from Interviews with Blacks, Mexicans, Americans, and Whites." In M. A. Young Rifai (ed.): *Justice and Older Americans*, Lexington, Mass.: Lexington Books, Heath.

Rathbone-McCuan, E.
    1980   "Elderly Victims of Family Violence and Neglect." *Social Casework* 61 (5): 296–304.

Reiman, J. H.
    1976   "Aging as Victimization: Reflections on the American Way of (ending) Life." In J. Goldsmith and S. S. Goldsmith (eds.), *Crime and the Elderly*. Lexington, Mass.: Lexington Books, Heath.

Reppetto, T. A.
    1974   *Residential Crime*. Cambridge, Mass.: Ballinger.

Rifai, M. A. (ed.)
    1977a   *Justice and Older Americans*. Lexington, Mass.: Lexington Books, Heath.

Rifai, M. A.
    1977b   "Perspectives on Justice and Older Americans." In M. A. Young Rifai (ed.): *Justice and Older Americans*, Lexington, Mass.: Lexington Books, Heath.

Rifai, M. A., and Ames, S. A.
    1977   "Social victimization of Older People: A Process of Social Exchange." In M. A. Young Rifai (ed.): *Justice and Older Americans*. Lexington, Mass.: Lexington Books, Heath.

Rosenfeld, F. H.
    1981   "Criminal Victimization of the Elderly." In D. Lester (ed.), *The Elderly Victim of Crime*. Springfield, Illinois: Charles C. Thomas Publisher.

Sante et Bien-etre Canada et Statistique Canada
    1981   *La santé des Canadiens — Rapport de l'enquête sur la santé des Canadiens.* Approvisionnements et Services Canada, Ottawa, Ontario.

Shanas, E.
    1979   "The Family as a Social Support System in Old Age." *Gerontologist* 19.

Shell, D. J.
    1982   *Protection of the Elderly: A Study of Elder Abuse.* Manitoba Council on Aging. Winnipeg, Manitoba: Manitoba Association on Gerontology.

Shotland, R. L., S. C. Hayward *et al.*
    1979   "Fear of Crime in Residential Communities." *Criminology* 17 (1): 34–45.

Silverman, R. and L. W. Kennedy
    1983   Age, Perception of Social Diversity and Fear of Crime. Discussion Paper 2. Centre for Criminological Research. Population Research Laboratory, Department of Sociology, University of Alberta: Edmonton.

Silverman, R., and V. Sacco
    1980   *Crime Prevention Through Mass Media: An Evaluation.* Report prepared for the Solicitor General of Canada.

Skogan, W. G.
    1977   "Public Policy and the Fear of Crime in Large American Cities." In J. A. Gardiner (ed.), *Public Law and Public Policy.* New York: Praeger.
    1978   *Victimization surveys and criminal justice planning.* United States Department of Justice: National Institute of Law Enforcement and Criminal Justice.
    1980   Adjusting Rates of Victimization for Exposure to Risk, to Understand the Crime Problems of the Elderly. Paper presented at the American Society of Criminology, San Francisco, Calif. (November).
    1983   "La sécurité dans les grandes villes américaines." *Revue Internationale de Criminologie et de Police Technique.* XXXVI (4): 24–35.

Skogan, W., and M. Maxfield
    1981   *Coping With Crime: Individual and Neighborhood Reactions.* Beverly Hills: Sage.

Smith, R. J.
    1979   "Crime against the Elderly: Implications for Policy-Makers and Practitioners." *Security Systems Digest* 10 (November 5).

Solicitor General. Canada
    1983   "Canadian Urban Victimization Survey." Bulletin No. 1: Victims of Crime. Ottawa: Research and Statistics Group, Canada.
    1984   "Canadian Urban Victimization Survey." Bulletin No. 2: Reported Crimes. Ottawa: Research and Statistics Group, Canada.
    1984   "Canadian Urban Victimization Survey." Bulletin No. 3: Crime Prevention: Awareness and Practice. Ottawa. Research and Statistics Group, Canada.
    1984   "Cost of Crime to Victims: Preliminary Findings of the Canadian Urban Victimization Survey." Statistics Division No. 1984–40. Ottawa: Programs Branch User Report.
    1984   "Discussion Aid on Abuse of the Elderly." Statistics Division No. 1984–44. Ottawa: Programs Branch User Report.

1984   "Preliminary Findings of the Canadian Urban Victimization Survey." Statistics Division No. 1984–51. Ottawa: Programs Branch User Report.

1984   "Who are the Victims?" Statistics Division No. 1984–38. Ottawa: Programs Branch User Report.

1985a   "Canadian Urban Victimization Survey." Bulletin No. 4: Female Victims of Crime. Ottawa. Research and Statistics Group, Canada.

1985b   "Canadian Urban Victimization Survey." Bulletin No. 5: Cost of Crime to Victims. Ottawa: Ministry Secretariat/Programs Branch, Canada.

1985c   "Canadian Urban Victimization Survey." Bulletin No. 6: Criminal Victimization of Elderly Canadians. Ottawa. Ministry Secretariat/Programs Branch, Canada.

Stafford, M. C. and O. R. Galle

1984   "Victimization Rates, Exposure to Risk and Fear of Crime." *Criminology* 22 (2/May 1984): 173–185.

Stannard, C. I.

1973   "Old Folks and Dirty Works: The Social Conditions for Patient Abuse in a Nursing Home." *Social Problems* 20 (3): 329–342.

Statistics Canada

1979   Catalogue Number 91–520. Ottawa: Minister of Supply and Services Canada.

1982   *1981 Census of Canada*. Ottawa, Ontario: Minister of Supply and Services Canada.

1984   *The Elderly in Canada*. Ottawa. Minister of Supply and Services. Catalogue 99–932.

1985   *Canadian Crime Statistics 1985*. Ottawa: Minister of Supply and Services Canada. Catalogue 85–205.

1986   *Income Distribution by Size in Canada*. 1984. Ottawa. Minister of Supply and Services Canada. Catalogue 13–207.

Steinmetz, S. K.

1978   "Battered Parents." *Society* 15 (5/July/August): 54–55.

1981   "Elder Abuse." *Aging*. (January/February): 6–10.

1983   Dependency, Stress, and Violence Between Middle Aged Caregivers and Their Elderly Parents. Pp. 134–150 in J. I. Kosberg (ed.), *Abuse and Maltreatment of the Elderly: Causes and Interventions*: Boston, Bristol, London: John Wright- PSG Inc.

Stinchcombe, L. A., R. Adams, C. A. Heimer, K. L. Scheppele, T. W. Smith, and D. G. Taylor

1980   *Crime and Punishment: Changing Attitudes in America*, San Francisco-London-Washington: Jossey-Boss Publishers.

Strauss, M. A., R. J. Gelles, and S. K. Steinmetz

1980   *Behind Closed Doors*. Garden City, NY: Anchor.

Streuer, J., and Austin, E.

1980   "Family Abuse of the Elderly." *Journal of the Geriatrics Society* 28: 372–375.

Sundeen, R.

1977   "The Fear of Crime and Urban Elderly." M. Young Rifai, (ed.).*Justice and Older Americans*, Lexington, Mass.: Lexington Books, Heath.

Sundeen, R., and J. Mathieu
1976a "The Fear of Crime and its Consequences among Elderly in Three Urban Communities," *The Gerontologist* 16 (3): 211–219.
1976b "The Urban Elderly: Environments of Fear." In Goldsmith, J. and S. S. Goldsmith (eds.), *Crime and the Elderly*. Lexington, Mass.: Lexington Books, Heath.

Teski, M.
1981 "Environment, Crime, and the Elderly." In Lester D. (ed.): *The Elderly Victim of Crime*, Springfield, Illinois: Charles C. Thomas, Publisher.

Therrier, B. and P. Bouchard
1983 *Les conditions de vie des personnes âgées à domicile*. Ministère des Affaires sociales du Québec. Direction de l'évaluation des programmes. Québec: Services des études sociales.

Time Magazine
1976 *The Elderly: Prisoners of Fear*. September 19, p. 21.

Tremblay, O.
1984 "Victimes aux cheveux blancs." *Justice*, VI (4/Avril): 24–30.

U.S. Congress, House
1977 "Select Committee on Aging." *In Search of Security: A National Perspective on Elderly Crime Victimization*, Washington: USGPO.

U.S. Congress, Senate
1972 *Special Committee on Aging: Hearing before the Sub-committee on Housing for the Elderly*, 92e Cong., 1st sess., October.

U.S. Department of Justice
1977 *Public Opinion About Crime: The Attitudes of Victims and Non-Victims in Selected Cities*, Washington, DC.: U.S. Government Printing Office.

Ward, R. A.
1979 *The Aging Experience: An Introduction to Social Gerontology*, New York: J. P. Lippincott Co.

Warr, M.
1984 "Fear of Victimization: Why are Women and the Elderly more Afraid." *Social Science Quarterly*, 65 (3/September).

Warr, M. and M. Stafford
1982 "Fear of Victimization: A Look at the Proximate Causes. *Social Forces* 61 (4): 1033–1043.

Winchester, S., and H. Jackson
1982 *Residential Burglary: The Limits of Prevention*. London. H.M.S.O.: Home Office Research Study No. 74.

Wolfgang, M. E.
1958 *Patterns in Criminal Homicide*. Philadelphia: University of Pennsylvania Press.

Yin, P.
1980 "Fear of Crime Among the Elderly: Some Issues and Suggestions." *Social Problems* 27 (4): 492–504.
1982 "Fear of Crime as a Problem for the Elderly." *Social Problems*, 30 (2/December): 240–246.

1985   *Victimization and the Aged*. Springfield, Illinois: Charles C. Thomas, Publisher.
Zay, N. et Blossom T. Wigdor
   1985   *La planification de la retraite*. Manuel de référence complet à l'intention des Canadiens. Toronto/Montréal: Editions Grosvenor Inc.

INDEX